Anton's Festive Salsas

By Anton Anderssen

By Anton Anderssen

Published in Warren, Michigan by

 Hartforth Publications

4177 Garrick Ave
Warren Michigan 48091
Phone 586 757 4177
Fax 313 557 6367
http://hartforth.freeyellow.com
Email: Hartforth@aol.com
International Standard Book Number:
0 9666119 1 8
Printed in the United States
First Edition

Romero Anton Montalban-Anderssen

The author, Romero Anton Montalban-Anderssen is a proud to be a full member of the Southeastern Cherokee Council.

This book is dedicated to my family. With the help of my sister, Lisa Cortéz, who supplied many of the recipes for this book, it is hoped that our family will remember its Native American Heritage, and that my nephews Nicolás Cortéz and Austin Cortéz will endeavor to learn as much as possible about their Native American Cherokee and their Hispanic heritage. In honor of my ancestral grandmothers who handed down many Cherokee traditions to our family, I dedicate this book. In honor of all my ancestors who lived in Alabama, Georgia, and Florida when those states still were part of Spain, I dedicate this book, and recognize the important contributions that Hispanic culture has shared with us. In honor of John Vulpe, who inspires me to learn all I can about great foods, I dedicate this book. In honor of Gary Mott, who awakened my taste buds to Tex-Mex cuisine, I dedicate this book. In honor of my nephew Nathan, and my brothers Jim and Roger, who helped me realize just how much we Americans love peppers in our foods, I dedicate this book. In honor of all my Native American Cherokee "family" in the Southeastern Cherokee Council, who inspire me to honor and remember my Native American heritage, I dedicate this book. In honor of the administrators at community education centers, e.g. Warren Consolidated Schools, Royal Oak Neighborhood Schools, HFCC, Southfield Center for the Arts, et al., who promote cultural diversity and lifelong learning, I dedicate this book.

Introduction

This book contains salsa recipes from the Southwest US and around the world. Many of these salsas have been Native American Indian dishes for hundreds of years. These recipes are comprised chiefly of foods indigenous to the Americas. Many come from Native American Indian reservations in Arizona, California, New Mexico, and from Anton's Cherokee grandmothers. Anton is a tribally registered Cherokee, and is proud to share those Native American salsas which are traditional Native American Indian fare. Other salsa recipes in this book were discovered as Anton trekked the planet in search of tasty peppers and salsas so you might enjoy these festive culinary sensations!

Salsas are popular year-round and can help create a lively party atmosphere. In this book you will find 200 salsa recipes to delight and awaken your senses. Be sure to read important information about the heat factors associated with various peppers. Some peppers can cause serious injury or death to sensitive individuals.

Chiles and Salsas

Chiles have been with us for some 8,000 years (c. 6200 BC). Ancient peoples buried chiles with the deceased, and indigenous people to the Americas gathered chiles around their canoes to ward off evils water creatures. By 1650 chiles had found their way to all corners of the world.

The first method for determining the heat level of a chile was developed in 1912 by Dr. Wilbur Scoville, a chemist for the Parke Davis Company. He devised the Scoville Organoleptic Test, which was highly subjective and was replaced by scientific testing in 1980. The results of these new tests are still coded in Scoville units (not in Wilbur units, to the chagrin of Mr. Ed), which measure the amount of capsaicin... N-Vanillyl-8-methyl-6(E)-noneamide in peppers. The capsaicin is concentrated in the veins and flesh of the pepper.

The #1 Factor that contributes to a chile's heat level is its maturity. While capsaicin is present at the beginning of the fruit's development, the amount of capsaicin increases as the chile matures.

Eating chiles is addicting. When capsaicin comes in contact with the nerves in your mouth, pain signals are sent to the brain. Subsequently, the brain releases endorphins, natural painkillers, that create a feeling euphoria. The more spicy food ingested the more endorphins released.

Choose your chiles which are firm and have a smooth glossy surface. Ripe (red) peppers are sweeter than the green ones, they taste less acidic, and are more supple.

Wear rubber gloves when cutting chiles. When disposing seeds down the drain, run cold water only.

To neutralize hot pepper taste in your mouth, eat dairy products like milk, ice cream, or yogurt. If that doesn't work, rub peanut butter around in your mouth. Water or beer will only make the heat worse.

Mild Peppers

Ancho: This chile is 3 to 4 inches wide. It has a rating of 1,000 Scoville units. The Ancho will add a sweet plum/raisin like flavor to dishes. It is most commonly used in sauces or purees. Also known as Poblano when fresh (Ancho when dried)

Anaheim: This chile has a rating of 1,200 Scoville units.

Bell Peppers / Sweet Italian peppers: These are the most commonly identifiable peppers, and have zero to 150 Scoville units. They are great in salads, as they come in various colors: yellow, orange, green, red, and black.

Cascabel: This chile is round in shape. It has a rating of 3,000 Scoville units. The cascabel will add a deep, nutty flavor to dishes. It is great in salsas and sauces.

Guajillo: This chile is 4-6 inches long and 1 inch wide. The guajillo is 5,000 Scoville units and will add a sweet flavor with hints of berry to your recipes. It is most often used in stews and sauces.

New Mexican: This chile is 6 inches long by 1 inch wide and has a clear, sweet, earthy flavor. It measures 1,000 Scoville units. The New Mexican chile is often used in salsas or added to soups.

Pasilla: The pasilla chile is about 6 inches long by 1 inch wide and has a complex, deep, smoky raisin flavor . Its Scoville rating is 2,500 units. The pasilla is often used in salsas and stews.

Poblano: This chile has a rating of 2,000 to 3,000 Scoville units.

Medium Peppers

Chipotle: The chipotle, also known as the smoked Jalapeño, is 2 inches long and 1/2 inch wide. This wrinkled brown and red chili is a Jalapeño pepper that has been mesquite smoked and dried. It has a unique toasted smoky flavor. The chipotle rates 10,000 Scoville units. It is great in all types of food from soups to salsas and more.

Jalapeño: Jalapeño chiles are the most popular peppers. They have a sharp pungent flavor The Jalapeño chile measures 10,000 Scoville heat units.

Serrano: This chile has a rating of 16,000 Scoville units. It is popular in salsa verde recipes at Mexican restaurants.

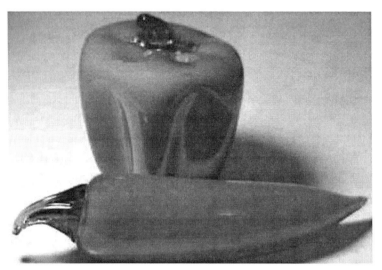

Hot Peppers

Cayenne: This chile has an acidic flavor. It has a rating of 35,000 Scoville units.

Chile de Arbol: This chile is 2 to 3 inches long and bright-to-deep red. The chile de arbol is 25,000 Scoville units. It will add a natural, grassy flavor to dishes. In pod form the de arbol is often used to flavor oils and vinegars. As a powder the de arbol is great in soups and chilis.

Japone: The japone chile is 1 to 2 inches long and 1/2 inch wide. It has a biting taste and measures 25,000 Scoville units. It will add pure heat to your dishes. It is added to many Oriental dishes, and has a toasty, dried berry flavor.

Pequin: The pequin is the smallest chile of all, about 1/3 inch long and wide. It is hot, measuring at 75,000 Scoville units. The pequin has a complex, smoky, citrus, nutty flavor.

Red Amazon: The red amazon, also referred to as the Tabasco chile, is 1 inch long by 1/2 inch wide. It has a light, fiery flavor with hints of celery. It measures 75,000 Scoville units. This chile is great in soups, salads, and sauces.

Tabasco: This chile has a rating of 35,000 Scoville units. It is owned by the company that makes the sauce.

Thai, pequin, chiltepin chiles have a rating of 50,000 to 75,000 Scoville units.

Dangerously Hot Peppers

Habañero: The Habañero chile is the hottest family of chiles in the world. It is 1 1/2 inches long and 1/2 inch wide. It has a rating of 300,000 Scoville units. Used in moderation, this chile is extremely flavorful. It will add a light, citrus flavor to your recipes. The Habañero chile is a great compliment to chutneys, stir frys, soups, or even pizza! According to the Guiness Book of World Records, the Red Savina Habañero has a rating of 570,000 Scoville units.

Scotch Bonnet: The scotch bonnet and the Habañero chile are of the same species but not of the same cultivar. It has a tropical and fruity flavor. This chile has a rating of 100,000 to 200,000 Scoville units. The scotch bonnet is used in jerk sauces and Caribbean salsas.

Salsas

Salsa is a Spanish word for sauce, however in *GringoLandia* it is a generic word for a variety of different chunky, usually highly seasoned mixtures. This yummy dip can be made at home from fresh ingredients. A huge variety of tomato-laden salsa recipes are floating around, and trendy fruit salsas based on papaya, mango and peaches -- or vegetable salsas based on corn and black beans -- are growing rapidly in popularity. Salsa now is now more popular than even catsup as a condiment.

Salsa is more than just a dip. It is spicy, fresh, full of chunks and fat free. When it comes to today's culinary tastes, salsa pushes all the right buttons.

Some salsas taste better than others and some are just different. You'll note an important distinction between fresh raw salsa (salsa cruda) and cooked salsa (salsa de cocina). Both must be refrigerated, and beware that bacteria love salsa too! Salsa Tips

The type of tomato you choose will greatly affect the salsa

you create. Paste tomatoes, such as Romas, are more solid

and create thicker salsas than your large slicing tomatoes. Slicing tomatoes create a watery salsa. There are at least 10,000 varieties of tomatoes. Overripe tomatoes will create an appalling salsa. Never refrigerate a tomato that is not fully red or ripe! Cold temperatures destroy flavor and stop the ripening process. Once fully ripe, a tomato can be refrigerated, but only for a few days; any longer results in flavor deterioration.

In salsa recipes, green tomatoes or tomatillos (Mexican husk tomatoes) can be substituted for red tomatoes or mixed into them. You don't have to peel or seed tomatillos, but you have to remove the dry outer husk.

Chiles range from sweet to fiery in taste. As a rule of thumb, the bigger the pepper, the milder the flavor. Anaheim, Ancho, College, Colorado and Hungarian Yellow Wax are mild varieties. Use mild peppers in recipes requiring long green chilies.

Small, hot peppers add a lot of punch to salsas. Jalapeño is the most popular hot pepper. You will also see Serrano, Cayenne, Habañero and Tabasco. Always wear rubber gloves when you cut these peppers because they burn your skin. Do not touch your face, particularly near your eyes or nose, when you are working with hot chilies. Substitute with bell peppers when you need a milder flavor. If you want more pepper flavor in a recipe, don't add more peppers – instead switch to a hotter pepper.

Add acidic ingredients to preserve salsa, like bottled lemon juice or vinegar.

Cilantro (coriander) and cumin often are ingredients in salsa, but you can leave these out for a milder taste. For stronger cilantro taste, use the herb fresh. Cilantro, Chinese parsley and fresh coriander leaves are different names for the same plant. Cilantro usually refers to the fresh leaves used as an herb, and coriander to the seeds used as a spice. They are quite different in flavor, can not be used as substitutes for one another. The roots are also eaten as a vegetable. Coriander is mentioned as an aphrodisiac in The Tales of the Arabian Nights.

Salsa Ingredients

When you think of salsa, you probably first think of the **tomato based** type. This is common in Mexico, central America, and in the Southwest US. This type contains tomatoes, onions and chiles as its major ingredients. They may contain ripe red and unripe green tomatoes, yellow, Italian plum, Roma tomatoes or cherry varieties. They may also contain tomatillos.

You can use fresh, dried, or canned tomatoes. It is increasingly popular to roast tomatoes along with vegetables for interesting salsa textures (leave in the skins). You can substitute or embellish any dish that calls for a tomato product with a tomato salsa – such as adding some to spaghetti. We love our friend the onion, but you can use any **vegetable** as the centerpiece of a salsa, such as corn, dried beans and peas, chayote squash, artichokes, radishes, sweet potatoes or eggplant. These salsas can be used in lieu of a vegetable at dinner, or they can be a relish for sandwiches. Vegetable salsas can also be used as salads.

Fruit salsas combine sweet/tart or hot/sweet combinations, and are made from just about any fruit. You can create tropical blends from bananas, pineapples, mangos and papayas. Use fresh, not frozen fruits. Salsas add a splash of color to any meal.

Salsa Categories

Salsa falls into major categories.

Genuine Mexican red salsa is deep red, based on tomatoes, with an apparent, yet balanced taste of cilantro. Cumin often is used, but it should not dominate. Onions should be apparent, but not overbearing. Hotness can vary from mild to 'blow the fire outa yer mouth,' although too-hot generally is discouraged when making Mexican red salsa. This variety often is served warm to provide full flavor. Serve with white or yellow corn tortilla chips.

Genuine Mexican green salsa must, by definition, be green. The color comes solely from using green peppers. A true Jalapeño pepper, and lots of it, is preferred. Cilantro and onion balance the flavor. Hotness is on the extreme upper end of the spectrum. Serve it with lots of cold beer. The style of chips is irrelevant.

Tex-Mex salsa is much like genuine Mexican red salsa, except it is less restrictive and the use of cilantro is optional. Expect a bold tomato flavor, perhaps with a little cumin. It matters little what kind of peppers are used because the strong tomato flavor likely will drown out any distinctive pepper flavor. Tex-Mex salsa isn't as hot as Mexican red salsa, so folks north of Dallas can enjoy it, too. Serve it at any temperature, because the word is that those who like this style usually don't know any better anyway. Tex-Mex salsa can be served with any type of chip.

Border green salsa most often is found in genuine Mexican restaurants. Tomatillos are the primary source of color and flavor for this typically mild salsa. This salsa should be light green in color and creamy in texture, without tomatoes or onions. Poblano peppers are acceptable, in addition to Serrano and a tiny bit of Jalapeño.

Fruit Salsas are festive dishes to add to all kinds of meat dishes. Alternatively, **Vegetable Salsas** are equally yummy!

Salsa Recipes

1   AVOCADO TOMATO SALSA

2 medium ripe avocados, peeled and cubed
1 large tomato diced
⅓ cup minced onion
1 lime juice of
1 teaspoon pepper sauce

1 1/2 tablespoons vegetable oil
1 tablespoon chopped fresh cilantro
1/3 cup finely chopped green onions
2 teaspoons minced ginger

2   HOT SALSA

3 medium tomatoes
3 to 4 Jalapeño peppers
onion your choice

oregano dash
salt and pepper

In saucepan boil tomatoes and peppers. Drain water and remove skin from tomatoes. Put in blender with remaining ingredients and blend for a minute or until smooth, unless you prefer your salsa chunky. Serve with tortilla chips.

3   Roma SALSA

8 Roma tomatoes, finely chopped
8 tomatoes, finely chopped
1 bunch cilantro, finely chopped
1 medium red onion, finely chopped
1 clove garlic, minced

2 celery finely, chopped
2 small Jalapeño peppers
1 green chili pepper or to taste
1 Serrano pepper or to taste
1 teaspoon salt
red cayenne pepper to taste
black pepper to taste

Combine first six ingredients in a large bowl and mix well. Chop the peppers finely and add to large bowl. Mix salsa well. Add the spices and mix. Let chill in refrigerator for at least 1 hour for flavor to combine.

4   BASIC GREEN MEXICAN SALSA

8 green tomatillo
1/2 large onion

fresh green chilies Serranos
quantity as you want

1 clove garlic   10 leaves of cilantro optional
salt and pepper

Peel the green tomatillo if they still have the dry skin. In a
boiling water cook the tomatillo and chilies Serranos for 1 or 2
minutes. Ground all the ingredients. You can use this fresh salsa for
tacos or quesadillas or if you want you can cook it: In a sauce pan add
a little amount of vegetable oil and when it will be warm add the
"salsa", cook for 20 minutes or more.

5   BLACK BEAN AND CORN SALSA

1 cup black beans cooked,   ½ cup diced tomato
cooled and drained   4 tablespoons shallots minced
¼ cup diced red onion   4 tablespoons garlic minced
3-4 Jalapeños, minced   4 ounces rice wine vinegar or
1 cup corn kernels   to taste
½ cup green onion chopped   salt and pepper to taste
½ cup red bell pepper diced

Toss beans with onion, Jalapeño, corn, green onion, bell pepper,
tomato, shallots, garlic, vinegar, salt and pepper. Let sit for a little
while before serving, or refrigerate covered.

6   CARIBBEAN SALSA

1 cup pineapple chopped   ½ cup red onion chopped
1 cup mango peeled chopped   ¼ cup cilantro fresh minced
1 cup red bell pepper chopped   1 teaspoon lemon juice
2/3 cup kiwi peeled chopped

7   CHIPOTLE SALSA

30 each dried chipotle chilies   12 each garlic cloves, peeled
or 3 cup chipotle chilies.   2 tablespoon salt
8 each ripe Roma tomatoes,   ½ teaspoon black pepper,
cored   freshly ground

Combine all of the ingredients in a medium saucepan. Bring to a boil,
reduce to a simmer and cook, uncovered, for about 20 minutes. The
liquid should be reduced by one-third and the tomato skins should be
falling off. Set aside to cool. Pour the mixture into a blender or a food
processor fitted with the metal blade. Puree until smooth and then
pass through a strainer. Serve chilled. Chipotle salsa can be stored in
the refrigerator for up to 5 days or frozen.

8   COOL PAPAYA SALSA

¾ cup papaya, peeled and   ¼ cup green bell pepper,
diced   diced
¼ cup red onion, diced

2 tablespoon cilantro leaves, chopped

2 tablespoon lime juice
1 pinch salt and pepper

9   EVIL JUNGLE PRINCE SALSA

3 large ripe tomatoes
⅓ cup finely chopped white onions
¼ cup fresh orange juice
1 or 2 fresh Habañero chilies, stemmed and coarsely chopped
1 tablespoon fresh lime juice

1 ½ teaspoon salt
⅔ cup finely diced seedless cucumber
⅔ cup finely diced red radish
⅔ cup finely diced jicama root
⅓ cup finely chopped cilantro
3 tablespoon finely chopped fresh mint

Trim and halve the tomatoes. Gently squeeze out and discard the seeds and juice. Chop the tomatoes. In a food processor, combine the tomatoes, onions, orange juice, Habañero, lime juice, and salt and process until fairly smooth. Transfer the puree to a bowl and stir in the diced cucumber, radish, jicama, cilantro and mint. Adjust the seasoning. Refrigerate for at least 30 minutes before serving. The salsa can be prepared up to 1 day in advance.

10   FIERY HOT SALSA

3 medium tomatoes
1 medium onion
2 tablespoon cilantro, chopped
1 pinch oregano
1 dash salt

2 each yellow bell peppers
3 each Habañero peppers or Jalapeño peppers
¼ each green bell pepper
¼ each yellow bell pepper
juice of 1 lime

11   FRESH PEACH SALSA

3 ½ cups diced peeled peaches
¼ cup diced red onion
2 tablespoons finely chopped fresh cilantro

1 tablespoon minced seeded Jalapeño pepper
2 tablespoons rice vinegar
1 teaspoon lemon juice
1 clove garlic minced

12   FRESH TOMATO AND AVOCADO SALSA

2 large tomatoes, chopped
1 Jalapeño chili, seeded and finely chopped
2 tablespoons sliced green onions

2 tablespoons chopped fresh cilantro
2 tablespoons balsamic vinegar
¼ teaspoon salt
1 small avocado diced

13 MEXICAN SALSA FRIA

2 pound peeled ripe tomatoes, chopped

3 tablespoon olive oil
3 tablespoon wine vinegar

1 cup chopped sweet onions
salt to taste
freshly ground pepper to taste
coriander to taste

4 or 5 canned green chilies, chopped
1 can Mexican tomatillo, chopped

Combine all ingredients and serve very cold. The coriander, sometimes known as cilantro, or Chinese parsley, should be fresh; if not available, substitute oregano.

14 CANTELOUPE SALSA

1 ripe cantaloupe
½ sweet red pepper seeded
2 Serrano chilies
2 tablespoons finely chopped cilantro

1 tablespoon unseasoned rice vinegar
1 juice of one lime
¼ cup sugar to taste

15 MEXICAN CORN SALSA

11 ounce corn, whole kernel drained
2 medium tomatoes, Roma, seeded, diced
4 ounce chilies, green, chopped un-drained
¼ cup onions, green, sliced

1 tablespoon juice, lemon
1 tablespoon cilantro, minced
1 small pepper, Jalapeño, finely chopped
1 small garlic, clove, minced
¼ teaspoon salt

16 MILD FRESH SALSA

3 tomatoes finely chopped
½ teaspoon salt
½ cup finely chopped fresh cilantro or parsley
2 or 3 cloves garlic minced

1 4oz can chopped green chilies
½ cup sliced green onions
¼ teaspoon pepper

17 TOMATO PAPAYA MACADAMIA NUT SALSA

6 tomatoes, blanched, peeled, seeded, and chopped
1 papaya, peeled, seeded, and diced
½ red onion, diced
¼ cup macadamia nuts, toasted and chopped

2 tablespoon mint, chopped
1 tablespoon cilantro, chopped
¼ cup fresh lime juice
¼ cup olive oil

18 PAPAYA AVOCADO SALSA

2 tablespoons fresh lemon juice
½ teaspoon salt
¼ teaspoon cumin

½ cup sweet onion small cubed
½ cup yellow pepper small cubed

½ cup papaya small cubed
½ cup avocado small cubed

2 tablespoons chopped cilantro

Mix first three ingredients in a large bowl. Cube the vegetables and fruits in small cubes. Twist and chop the cilantro. Add remaining ingredients to lemon, salt and cumin mixture. Mix entire recipe. Serve over fish and chicken or with low-fat chips.

19 PINEAPPLE SALSA

½ cup pineapple diced in small pieces
½ cup firm ripe mango
½ cup cucumber diced and peeled
⅓ cup red bell pepper diced
⅓ cup tomato diced

3 tablespoon green onion or chives, finely chopped
3 tablespoon cilantro or 1 teaspoon mint
juice of 2 limes
hawaiian chili pepper or Jalapeño to taste

20 PINTO BEAN CHILE SALSA

¾ cup pinto beans dried
1 teaspoon salt
3 arbol chilies with seeds
3 pasilla chilies seeded
2 Jalapeño chilies for garnish
2 chipotle chilies
⅓ onion diced

½ cup olive oil
2 garlic cloves roasted
2 Roma tomatoes blackened
¾ cup dark beer
1 tablespoon peanut oil
1 teaspoon cider vinegar

Wash and drain beans, place in a large pot and cover with water. Cook until soft, for about 1 ½ to 2 hours,. Drain and transfer to a mixing bowl. Add the salt. Toast the arbol and pasilla chilies together. Re-hydrate all dried chiles in one cup of warm water. If using canned or fresh, omit this step. Drain and set aside. Roast and peel Jalapeño chilies, seed, dice and set aside. Heat olive oil and sauté the onion over medium-high heat until caramelized. Transfer to a blender along with the chilies (not the Jalapeño chilies), garlic, tomatoes, beer and puree. In a wok or large skillet, heat peanut oil until smoking hot and add the puree. Re-fry until reduced and thickened, this will take about 5 minutes. Transfer ¾ of this refried mixture to a mixing bowl and add beans and cider vinegar. Garnish with Jalapeño.

21 PLUM TOMATO SALSA WITH SHERRY VINEGAR

6 plum tomatoes, peeled, seeded, and cut into ½ inch dice
1 medium shallot, sliced thin

1 Serrano chile, seeded and sliced thin
2 tablespoon sherry vinegar
½ cup olive oil

½ teaspoon chopped fresh thyme
1 tablespoon chopped fresh cilantro

1 tablespoon chopped fresh parsley
salt and pepper to taste

22 GREEN CHILE SALSA

2 can whole tomatoes (16 ounces)
1 can green chilies (small) chopped
1 packet green onions
1 green chile, fresh
1 Jalapeño pepper, fresh
1 tomato, fresh

1 tablespoon vinegar
1 teaspoon sugar
salt and pepper, to taste
1 teaspoon garlic powder
1 teaspoon oregano
1 teaspoon cayenne pepper
1 teaspoon cumin
tortilla chips, crispy

Put 1 can of tomatoes in a blender. Pulse just enough to make a coarse sauce; this is the base of the salsa. Empty blender container into a large serving bowl. Coarsely chop the onions, tomatoes (canned and fresh), and peppers and add to the bowl along with the canned chilies. Add remainder of ingredients. Salt and pepper to taste. Stir to mix well. Serve as an appetizer with corn chips or to spice up your favorite Mexican dish.

23 ANCHO CHILI SALSA

8 chilies Anchos
½ cup red wine vinegar
1 onion
½ teaspoon salt

4 garlic cloves small
¼ cup queso fresco crumbled
½ cup olive oil

Toast chilies lightly, turning constantly so not to burn them. When cool, remove veins and seeds. Cut chilies into small pieces and chop onion and garlic finely. Mix chilies, onion, and garlic with oil, vinegar and salt. Let stand for approximately 2 hrs. To serve sprinkle with cheese.

24 SALSA DI SPINACI

1 cup olive oil
2 tablespoon lemon juice
2 tablespoon capers
½ pound spinach leaves, torn roughly

6 each lettuce leaves, torn roughly
salt and pepper
fresh pasta of your choice
sprigs continental parsley

Combine oil, lemon juice, capers, spinach and lettuce in a food processor. Blend until smooth. Season well with salt and pepper. Cook the pasta until al dente. Heat spinach puree slightly, being careful not to overcook or burn. Add to well drained pasta and combine. Garnish with parsley.

25 SALSA VERDE MEXICAN STYLE

½ medium onion, finely minced
1 tablespoon minced, fresh cilantro
1 Serrano or Jalapeño chile finely minced

26 BLAZING SALSA

2 each tomatoes, diced
1 each green pepper, seeded, diced
1 each medium onion, diced
1 tablespoon fresh cilantro, minced
3 each clove garlic, minced
4 each Jalapeño or Serrano peppers
2 teaspoon lime juice
2 teaspoon ground cumin
1 teaspoon dried oregano
1 teaspoon red salsa
¼ teaspoon black pepper
¼ teaspoon white pepper
¼ teaspoon salt
¼ teaspoon dried red pepper flakes
¼ teaspoon cayenne pepper
2 cup canned crushed tomatoes

Combine all the ingredients, except the crushed tomatoes, in a large bowl and mix well. Place three-quarters of the mixture in a food processor fitted with a steel blade and process for 5 seconds, creating a vegetable mash. Return the mash to the bowl, add the crushed tomatoes and blend well. Wrap the salsa tightly and chill for at least 1 hour, allowing the flavors to blend together. If kept refrigerated, salsa will keep for about 7 days.

27 SPICY CUCUMBER SALSA

2 whole cucumbers seedless
2 medium shallots peeled and minced
1 ½ tablespoon Jalapeño pepper minced
1 ½ cup fresh mint loosely packed chopped medium
2 tablespoon champagne wine vinegar
1 teaspoon salt
¼ teaspoon freshly ground black pepper
3 teaspoon olive oil

Peel cucumbers in strips for a striped effect. Cut in half lengthwise; remove any seeds. Cut crosswise into ⅛-inch slices. Combine cucumbers, shallots, Jalapeño and mint. In a small bowl, combine vinegar, salt and pepper. Gradually whisk in olive oil until combined. Pour over cucumbers and toss gently to combine.

28   SPICY SHRIMP AND AVOCADO SALSA

1 yellow bell pepper
1 red bell pepper
4 Roma tomatoes
6 tomatillo, husks removed
4 garlic cloves
1 small white onion, peeled
and quartered (6 ounce)
2 Jalapeños, stems removed
1 cup loose packed chopped
cilantro
¼ cup tomato juice
2 teaspoon coarse salt
2 teaspoon maple syrup (real
maple)
4 teaspoon fresh lime juice
2 avocados, peeled, seeded
and diced
1 pound cooked shrimp,
peeled and diced
tortilla chips

Remove stems from Bell peppers. Split peppers in half, lengthwise and lightly oil the skin. In an oven-proof pan, arrange peppers(skin-side up), tomatoes, tomatillo, garlic, onion and Jalapeños. Broil under high heat 10 to 15 minutes, or until skins of the peppers are charred and the tomatoes and tomatillo are blistered and soft. Allow vegetables to cool. Peel skin from peppers. In a food processor, combine broiled vegetables (including any liquid from the pan) with cilantro, tomato juice, salt, maple syrup and lime juice; blend to yield a coarse puree. Just before serving, add avocado and shrimp and mix well.

29   SWEET CORN SALSA

2 cup fresh corn kernels
3 tablespoon butter, cold, cut
into pieces
¼ cup seeded and diced
tomatoes
1 small Jalapeño pepper,
seeded and minced
2 tablespoon minced red
onion
2 tablespoon chopped cilantro
¼ cup rice vinegar
⅛ teaspoon freshly ground
black pepper
¼ teaspoon coarse salt

Cut raw kernels off cobs with a sharp knife. Combine all ingredients in a saucepan over high heat and stir while bringing salsa to a boil. When butter has melted completely and takes on the look of a light butter sauce, remove from heat and serve immediately. Use with chicken or lobster.

30   TOMATILLO APPLE SALSA

24 fresh tomatillo hulled and
chopped
3 medium tart apples peeled,
cored and finely chopped
½ cup sweet red pepper
chopped
½ cup cider vinegar
5 fresh/can Jalapeño peppers
seeded and finely chopped

¼ cup snipped fresh cilantro   ¼ cup Sugar

Combine tomatillo, apples, sweet pepper, vinegar, Jalapeño peppers, cilantro, sugar, and 1 teaspoon salt in a 4 to 6-quartt kettle. Bring to boil. Reduce heat and simmer, uncovered, 15 minutes. Ladle into hot, sterilized half-pint jars, leaving ½-inch headspace. Adjust lids. Process in boiling-water canner for 10 minutes.

31 TROPICAL FRUIT AND BLACK BEAN SALSA

½ cup pineapple diced	½ cup onions, red, chopped
½ cup mango diced	½ cup beans, black cooked
½ cup papaya diced	1 Jalapeño minced
½ cup onions, red, chopped	

32   CHOCOLATE SCOTCH BONNET SALSA

18 chocolate scotch bonnets seeded	1/2 teaspoon ground allspice
1 red kishinev pepper; seeded	1/8 teaspoon salt
1 garlic clove - peeled and sliced	1 tablespoon honey
1 teaspoon whole cumin	4 teaspoon Dutch cocoa powder
1 teaspoon whole coriander seed	1 cup dark rum
	1/2 cup fruity olive oil

In a dry pan, toast the cumin, coriander and garlic over high heat until the seeds begin to pop and smell swell. Remove from heat and grind with the salt in a mortar and pestle until you almost have a paste. Put the chiles, spice paste, allspice, honey, cocoa, rum and olive oil in a food processor and puree. When the sauce is quite smooth, Pour it into sterile glass bottles, cork and Refrigerate.

33   PLANTATION SALSA

1/2 cup molasses	1/4 cup Worcestershire sauce
1/2 cup prepared mustard	2 teaspoon Tabasco sauce
1/2 cup vinegar or lemon juice	1/2 teaspoon garlic powder

Blend molasses and prepared mustard; stir in remaining ingredients. Heat to boiling. Use for basting ribs or chicken.

34   SPICE ISLAND SALSA

1 papaya, ripe, chopped	1 tablespoon ginger, finely grated
1 onion, chopped	1/3 cup dark rum
2 garlic cloves, minced	1/3 cup lime juice
4 Habañeros, stemmed, seeded	2 1/2 teaspoon honey

1/8 teaspoon cardamom, ground	1/8 teaspoon turmeric, ground
1/8 teaspoon anise, ground	1 pinch nutmeg
1/8 teaspoon cloves, ground	1 pinch cinnamon
	1 pepper to taste

Combine all ingredients in blender and puree just until smooth, or about 1 minute, taking care not to over-blend or aerate. Pour into a saucepan and bring to a boil, then simmer gently, uncovered, for 10 minutes. Remove from heat and allow to cool before bottling. the sauce will keep for approximately 6 weeks in the refrigerator.

35 SALSA BORRACHO FOR ENCHILADAS

3 tablespoon butter	2 cup diced tomatoes
4 clove garlic, minced	2 tablespoon tomato paste
4 tablespoon chili powder	1/2 cup beer
4 Jalapeños, diced	

In non-aluminum pan, melt the butter over medium low heat. Add the garlic, chili powder, and Jalapeños. Sauté until the chili powder begins to foam. Add remaining ingredients and bring to a boil. Simmer for 5 minutes. Remove from heat.

36 YELLOW TOMATO SALSA

1 pound yellow tomatoes	1 tablespoon champagne (or white wine)
1 large shallot very finely minced	1 vinegar
1 large clove garlic very finely minced	2 whole Serrano chiles seeded and minced
2 tablespoon fresh cilantro very finely minced	2 teaspoon lime juice
	1 salt to taste
	1 tablespoon maple syrup

In a food processor, using the steel blade, process tomatoes until well chopped. Do not puree. Combine tomatoes and their juices with shallot, garlic, cilantro, vinegar, chilies, lime juice, and salt, mixing well. Add maple syrup, if needed, to balance flavor and sweeten slightly. Cover and Refrigerate for at least 2 hours or until very cold. For a crunchier, more typical salsa, put tomatoes through fine die of a food grinder.

37 SALSA ALMENDRA ROJA

1/2 cup almonds, slivered; toasted	8 ounce tomato sauce
1 cup onion; finely chopped	2 teaspoon paprika
1 each garlic clove; crushed	1 teaspoon red chiles, ground
2 teaspoon oil	1/4 teaspoon red pepper, ground

Place almonds in food processor work bowl fitted with steel blade or in blender container; cover and process until finely ground. Cook onion and garlic in oil over medium heat, stirring frequently, until onion is tender. Stir in remaining ingredients except almonds. heat to boiling; reduce heat. simmer for 1 minute stirring constantly; stir in almonds. Serve hot..

38   FOUR PEPPER MARGARITA SALSA

2 large cloves garlic
6 Jalapeños, seeds removed
2 teaspoon coarsely chopped
fresh parsley
4 tomatillos, quartered
6 plum tomatoes, diced
1/2 yellow onion, finely diced
one 4 inch Anaheim pepper,
seeded and diced
cilantro freshly chopped
1 teaspoon black pepper
1/2 teaspoon salt
juice of 1 lime
zest of half a lime
1 teaspoon tequila

In a food processor, finely chop garlic and Jalapeño peppers. Add tomatillos and chop again. Remove the mixture and Combine it with the remaining ingredients in a saucepan. Bring to a boil over medium heat and simmer for 5 minutes. Pack in a clean jar, cool and chill.

39   GARBANZO SALSA

1 can garbanzos (8 ounce)
1 cup cilantro, fresh
1/3 cup yogurt, low-fat,
unflavored

1/3 cup green onion, chopped
1/4 cup lime juice
salt to taste
pepper to taste

Drain garbanzos; whirl smooth in a food processor or blender with cilantro, yogurt, onions, and lime juice. Add salt and pepper to taste.

40   CHILE DE ARBOL SALSA

55 dried chiles de arbol
1 1/2 tablespoon sesame seeds
2 tablespoon shelled
pumpkinseeds pepitas
1/4 teaspoon cumin seeds or
1/4 teaspoon ground cumin

2 cloves or a big pinch ground
1 teaspoon dried oregano
1 teaspoon salt (scant)
2 large garlic cloves, peeled
and roughly chopped
3/4 cup cider vinegar

Stem the chiles, then roll them between your thumb and fingers, pressing gently to loosen the seeds inside. Break in half, shake out as many seeds as possible, then place in a blender jar. Heat an ungreased skillet over medium-low. Measure in the sesame seeds and stir for several minutes as they brown and pop; scoop into the blender jar. Add the pumpkin seeds to the skillet. When the first one pops, stir constantly for several minutes, until all are golden and have popped up into a round shape. Pulverize the cumin, allspice and cloves in a mortar or spice grinder, then Add to the blender jar along with the oregano, salt, garlic and vinegar. Blend for several minutes, until the mixture is orange-red and feels quite smooth when a drop is rubbed between your fingers. Strain through a medium-mesh sieve, working the solids back and forth and pressing them firmly; there will be a fair amount of chile seeds, skins, sesame hulls and other debris to discard, but be careful that there is nothing liquid trapped within them. Stir in 3/4 cup water, then pour into a bottle, cover and Let stand for 24 hours before serving.

41   DREADED RED MENACE SALSA

3 dried Habañero chilies
1 tablespoon grated orange zest
1 cup raspberry vinegar
1 1/2 cup unsweetened raspberries
1/3 cup fresh orange juice

Combine the chiles, orange zest, and vinegar in a heavy non-reactive pot and bring to a boil. Reduce the vinegar to 1/3 cup, strain, and discard the solids. Return the vinegar to the saucepan. Puree the raspberries in a food processor fitted with a plastic dough blade. (a steel blade will crush the seeds, which will lend a bitter taste to the food). Then strain. Add the raspberry puree to the vinegar and simmer over low heat for 20 minutes. Cool to room temperature and Add the orange juice. The marinade will keep in the refrigerator in an airtight jar for 1 to 2 weeks.

42   WINTER SALSA WITH CHIPOTLE AND ORANGE

1 yellow bell pepper; chopped coarse
1 onion; chopped coarse
1/3 cup olive oil
1 navel orange
1 tablespoon minced canned chipotle chilies in adobo or to taste
a (28-ounce) can whole Italian plum tomatoes, seeded and drained well
1 small green bell pepper; diced
1 tablespoon chopped fresh coriander
1 tablespoon fresh lime juice

In a skillet sauté yellow bell pepper and onion in 1 1/2 tablespoons oil over moderately high heat until vegetables are just tender and beginning to brown. Grate 1/2 teaspoon zest from orange and reserve. Squeeze juice from orange. Add orange juice and chilies to onion mixture and cook 1 minute. Chop tomatoes coarse and in a bowl combine with reserved zest, onion mixture, green bell pepper, coriander, and lime juice. In a blender puree in a thin stream. Stir puree into salsa and transfer to a jar with a tight-fitting lid. Salsa keeps, covered and chilled, 1 week.

43 SPICY ISLAND SALSA

1 ripe papaya; peeled, seeded and coarsely chopped
1 medium yellow onion; coarsely chopped
2 medium garlic cloves; minced
4 scotch bonnet or Habañero peppers; stemmed and seeded
1-inch length of fresh ginger, peeled and coarsely chopped
1/3 cup dark rum

1/3 cup fresh lime juice
1/4 teaspoon salt
2 1/2 teaspoon honey
1/8 teaspoon cardamom
1/8 teaspoon anise
1/8 teaspoon cloves
1/8 teaspoon turmeric
1 pinch nutmeg
1 pinch cinnamon
freshly ground black pepper to taste

Combine all ingredients in blender and puree just until smooth, or about 1 minute (taking care not to over blend and aerate). Pour into a saucepan and bring to a boil, then simmer gently, uncovered, for 10 minutes. Remove from heat and allow to cool before bottling. Refrigerated, the sauce will keep approximately 6 weeks.

44 ONE FINE SALSA

1 pound butter
1/2 cup finely chopped onion
2 cloves garlic, minced
1/2 cup whiskey
1/4 cup Worcestershire sauce

1 teaspoon pepper
1 1/2 teaspoon dry mustard
1 teaspoon salt
1/4 teaspoon Tabasco

Melt butter in a saucepan; Add onion and garlic and cook slowly until is soft. Add remaining ingredients and beat to mix.

45 PINEAPPLE APRICOT SALSA

1 cup finely chopped peeled cored fresh pineapple
1/2 cup finely chopped red onion
1/2 cup apricot-pineapple preserves

1/4 cup chopped fresh cilantro
2 tablespoons fresh lime juice
1-1/2 tablespoons minced seeded jalapeño chili

Toss all ingredients in small bowl to blend. Season with salt and pepper. Can be made one day ahead. cover and chill.

46   PLUM CHILE SALSA

1 pound ripe purple or red plums (about 4 large), diced (about 3 cups)
1/3 cup minced red onion
1/2 cup finely chopped fresh cilantro

1/4 cup finely chopped fresh mint leaves
1 teaspoon minced seeded fresh jalapeño (wear rubber gloves)
1 tablespoon fresh lime juice
2 teaspoons sugar, or to taste

In a bowl, stir together the plums, onion, cilantro, mint, jalapeño, lime juice and sugar. salt and pepper to taste.

47   SEARING SALSA

2 tomatoes, diced
1 green bell pepper, seeded, diced
1 medium onion, diced
1 tablespoon minced fresh cilantro
3 cloves garlic, minced
4 jalapeño or Serrano peppers, seeded and minced
2 teaspoons lime juice

2 teaspoons ground cumin
1 teaspoon dried oregano
1 teaspoon Louisiana salsa
1/4 teaspoon black pepper
1/4 teaspoon white pepper
1/4 teaspoon salt
1/4 teaspoon dried red pepper flakes
1/4 teaspoon cayenne pepper
2 cups crushed tomatoes

Combine all the ingredients, except the crushed tomatoes, in a large bowl and Mix well. Place three-quarters of the mixture in a food processor and process briefly. Combine mixture and crushed tomatoes in a bowl, blend well. Cover tightly and chill for at least 1 hour.

48 AVOCADO AND KIWI SALSA

1 1/2 cups finely diced kiwi
1/3 cup chopped fresh cilantro
2 scallions or green onions, green part included, thinly sliced

1 or more chopped fresh Serrano chiles
1 tablespoon lime juice
2 medium-sized firm-ripe (not soft) avocados, diced
salt to taste

Mix the kiwi, cilantro, green onion, chiles, and lime juice in a bowl. Iif making a day ahead, do not Add the avocado until as soon as possible before serving, as it will turn brown if cut for more than a few hours ahead. The avocado should be tossed in gently, so that the cubes retain their shape.

49 SWEET POTATO SALSA

1 large North Carolina sweet
1 jalapeño, seeded and diced
potato, peeled and finely
diced
2 teaspoons salt
1 tablespoon olive oil
1 or 2 garlic cloves, minced
1 lime, juiced and rind grated

1 medium tomato, diced
1 teaspoon sugar
2 tablespoons red bell
pinch salt
pepper, diced
1 tablespoon cilantro,
chopped

Boil sweet potato in 1 quart of boiling water and salt for 1 or 2 minutes or until tender-crisp; cool. Combine all ingredients. Cover and Refrigerate (marinade) for at least 1 hour. Serve cold.

50 SWEET POTATO MARGARITA SALSA

1/2 cup mild onion, chopped
2 tablespoons cilantro,
chopped
2 cups fresh peaches, diced
3 tablespoons tequila,
orange(can also use fresh
mango)

liqueur or orange juice
1 to 2 tablespoons Serrano or
1 teaspoon lime rind, grated
hot chile, seeded and minced
1/4 teaspoon ground cumin

Combine all ingredients and blend well. Serve at room temperature. Use to top baked or grilled sweet potatoes or use as an accompaniment for chicken, ham, pork or shrimp.

51 WATERMELON SALSA

2 cups seeded watermelon
diced
1 cup honeydew melon diced
1 cup jicama peeled and diced

1 Anaheim or New Mexico
green chile roast, peeled, and
chopped
1 tablespoon fresh lime juice
2 tablespoons fresh chopped
cilantro

Mix all the ingredients together and Refrigerate for 1 hour before serving. This salsa will not keep well for more than a day

52 SWEET POTATO PECAN SALSA

1 1/2 pounds. sweet potatoes,
1/4 cup re-hydrated
cranberries, peeled and diced
1/2 teaspoon sugar
1/2 teaspoon salt

1/4 cup maple syrup
1/4 cup pecans, toasted
1 tablespoon red chile powder
(optional)
2 tablespoons orange juice

Boil sweet potatoes with sugar and salt for 4 minutes; Drain and cool. Combine sweet potatoes, pecans and cranberries; set aside. Cook maple syrup, chili powder and 1/4 cup water in saucepan over medium heat for 4 minutes or until reduced by half; cool and add orange juice.

53   BLACK BEAN CHILI RED ONION SALSA

4 cups dried black turtle beans
5 cloves garlic crushed
2 teaspoons ground cumin
2 1/4 teaspoons salt optional
black pepper to taste
2 teaspoons dried basil
1/2 teaspoon dried oregano
crushed red pepper or cayenne to taste
1 tablespoon fresh lime juice
2 medium green bell peppers chopped
2 tablespoons olive oil
1/2 cup tomato puree

2 cans diced green chilies (4 ounce)
red onion salsa recipe
cheddar cheese grated
Monterey jack cheese grated
sour cream for topping
red onion salsa
2 cups red onion chopped
1/2 cup fresh cilantro minced
2 cups fresh tomatoes minced
1/2 teaspoon salt optional
1 cup parsley minced
black pepper to taste

Soak beans in plenty of water for several hours or overnight. Drain off Soaking water and cook in fresh boiling water, partly covered, until tender (1-1/2 hours). Check water level during cooking; Add more as necessary. Transfer the cooked beans to a large kettle or saucepan. include about 2-3 cups of their cooking liquid. In a heavy skillet, sauté garlic, seasonings, lime juice, and bell peppers in olive oil over medium-low heat until the peppers are tender (for 10-15 minutes.) . Add these to the cooked beans, along with tomato puree and minced green chilies. Simmer uncovered over very low heat stirring now and then for about 45 minutes. (make the salsa during this time.) Serve topped with red onion salsa and, if desired, grated cheese and sour cream. red onion . Salsa directions: Combine all ingredients and Mix well. for a finer consistency, give the mixture a whirl or two in a food processor or blender.

54   PEAR GINGER SALSA

1 1/2 cups pears diced
1/3 diced red bell pepper
1/3 cup golden raisins
2 green onions thinly sliced
1 fresh or canned Jalapeño pepper minced

1 tablespoon white wine vinegar
2 teaspoons minced ginger
salt to taste

55 MANGO CHERRY SALSA

1 onion chopped
clove minced garlic
Jalapeños seeded and minced
juice of 2 limes
juice of 1 large. lemon

2 tablespoons vinegar
(preferably white wine or
cider)
1 pound fresh cherries seeded
and cut in half
1 jar mangos or 2 fresh cut in
1/2" cubes

Warm sauté pan over medium heat. Add enough oil to lightly cover bottom of pan, about 1 tablespoon. Add onions, peppers and garlic and sauté over medium heat until onions begin to collapse, for about 5 to 8 minutes. Add lime juice, lemon juice and vinegar. Bring to a boil, Add cherries and mangos. Simmer for 8 to 10 minutes, stirring occasionally. Remove from heat. Place in a serving bowl and chill. This may be served hot. If a smooth sauce is preferred, puree in food processor before chilling. This is served with grilled chicken or grilled or pan-seared fish.

56 SHRIMP GRAPEFRUIT AND AVOCADO SALSA

2 tablespoons ground dried
shrimp
1/2 cup fresh pink grapefruit
juice
2 tablespoons fresh lime juice
1 red Jalapeño finely diced
1 cup celery finely diced
2 medium green onions
chopped

2 medium avocados peeled
and sliced
2 teaspoons grated grapefruit
peel
1/4 teaspoon freshly ground
black pepper
1/2 teaspoon salt

Soak the ground shrimp in the grapefruit and lime juices for 10 minutes, then Mix with the rest of the ingredients. Serve at once.

57 APRICOT SALSA

1 cup fresh apricots diced
1/2 medium pineapple peeled
and diced
1/4 medium white onion diced
1 large avocado peeled, pitted
and diced
1 medium red bell pepper
diced

2 tablespoons fresh lime juice
1 tablespoon chopped fresh
cilantro
1/2 teaspoon salt
1/2 teaspoon freshly ground
black pepper

58 CHRISTMAS SALSA

2 medium navel oranges
whole
1 pound whole cranberries
washed well

2 Jalapeños chopped
1/4 cup chopped dried
apricots
1 tablespoon fresh cilantro

1/2 teaspoon ground cinnamon

1/4 teaspoon ground allspice
1/4 teaspoon ground ginger

Place the oranges, skin and all, in a food processor fitted with a steel blade and chop very fine. Then Add the cranberries, Jalapeños, apricots, and the spices and process again. Do not over chop as you want to retain the integrity of the cranberries, apricot, and Jalapeño. Refrigerate for at least 1 hour before serving

59 EGGPLANT SALSA

1 medium eggplant
1 tablespoon water
1 clove garlic minced
2 tablespoons balsamic vinegar
1 tablespoon fresh lemon juice

1/4 cup freshly grated parmesan cheese
1 tablespoon chopped fresh parsley or cilantro
1/2 teaspoon crushed pequin chile

Cut the stem off the eggplant, cut in half, then Place cut side down on a microwave-safe plate with 1 tablespoon water. Cover with plastic wrap and microwave on high for 5 minutes or until tender. Let cool, then peel and dice the eggplant. Place in a bowl with the rest of the ingredients, Mix well, and Refrigerate for 1 hour before serving. If you do not have a microwave, you can prick several holes in the eggplant with the tines of a fork and bake at 350 for 30 minutes. Let cool, then peel and chop.

60 CILANTRO LIME SALSA

1 small onion, finely chopped
1 cup chopped fresh cilantro
1/2 cup each chopped parsley and salad oil
6 tablespoon lime juice

3 tablespoon distilled white vinegar
2 cloves garlic, minced
1 Jalapeño or other small hot chile, stemmed, seeded and minced

61 JICAMA TOMATILLO SALSA

1 medium jicama, diced
2 pounds tomatillos (Mexican green tomatoes with a papery husk), seeded and diced
3 Jalapeños, seeded and finely diced
1 teaspoon chopped cilantro
1 teaspoon garlic (2 cloves, chopped)

1 teaspoon shallots (1 to 2 shallots), chopped
juice each of 1 lemon and 1 lime
salt and freshly ground black pepper to taste
2 ounces peanut oil
Jalapeño vinegar to taste

Prepare jicama; it can be diced finely or coarsely as desired 1/2 inch dice is typical. Place in a large mixing bowl. To prepare tomatillos, cut ends off, Remove insides and dice skins. Add to jicama in mixing bowl. Add Jalapeño, cilantro, garlic, and shallots. Mix all ingredients and adjust seasoning with lemon and lime juice, salt and pepper. Add peanut oil and toss to coat mixture. Correct spiciness and heat by adding Jalapeño vinegar.

62   WHITE SALSA

1 cup mayonnaise
1 cup sour cream
juice of 3 limes
4 cloves garlic, crushed
1.5 cup finely chopped fresh cilantro
1 (6-ounce) can pitted black olives, drained and coarsely chopped

1.5 cup finely chopped scallions
5 teaspoon hot pepper sauce, or to taste
salt and freshly ground white pepper to taste (optional)

In a medium bowl, Combine mayonnaise and sour cream. Add lime juice, garlic, cilantro, black olives, scallions, hot pepper sauce, salt and pepper. Taste and adjust seasonings if desired. Chill until serving.

63   RASPBERRY CHIPOTLE SALSA

2 tablespoon butter or olive oil
2 c Portabello mushrooms, sliced
1 small onion, chopped fine
1/2 cup water

1 teaspoon powdered beef, chicken or vegetable stock
1/4 cup port, red wine or sherry
1/2 -2/3 cup inferno raspberry chipotle

Heat butter and sauté onions and mushrooms on high for 2 - 3 minutes. Add port, stock and water and continue on high 5 minutes, until liquid is reduced and syrupy. Reduce to low, Add raspberry chipotle sauce and cook 2 minutes until heated through. Marinate 1 pound pork tenderloin, top sirloin or boneless chicken breasts in 1/3 cup smoked cayenne-chipotle for 2-4 hours, if possible. Remove from fridge one hour before cooking. grill on high 4-6 minutes on each side (depending on thickness) or till done. Slice along the bias and Serve with mashed potatoes and sauce.

64   SPICY CRANBERRY SALSA

1 teaspoonful olive oil
1 onion (6 ounce.), chopped
4 cloves garlic, minced

3 fresh Serrano chilies, stemmed and chopped
1 cup (about 5 ounce.) dried cranberries

2 firm-ripe tomatoes (about
1/2 pound., total), cored,
seeded and diced
1/2 cup apple cider

2 tablespoonfuls chopped
parsley
salt and pepper

In a 10- to 12-inch nonstick frying pan over medium heat, stir oil, onion, garlic, and chilies often until onion is lightly browned, about 5 minutes. Add cranberries, tomatoes, and cider. Simmer, stirring often, until cranberries are soft when pressed, about 5 minutes. Purée salsa mixture in a blender or food processor. Add parsley, and season salsa with salt and pepper to taste. Serve at room temperature

65   APPLE PEAR SALSA

2 tablespoon fresh lime juice
1/4 cup pineapple juice
3 anjou pears, unpeeled, diced
3 red delicious apples,
unpeeled and diced

2 tablespoon fresh mint, diced
3 Serrano chilies, seeded
minced

Mix the pineapple juice and lime juice in a large non-reactive bowl. Add the diced pears and apple, toss to combine juices with fruit and to prevent the fruit from turning brown. Add the chilies.

66   BANANA SALSA

2 large bananas
1/2 cup red bell pepper diced
1/2 cup green bell pepper
diced
1/2 scotch bonnet seed, dice
1 tablespoon ginger minced
1/4 cup cilantro chopped

3 tablespoon lime juice
2 tablespoon brown sugar,
packed
1/4 teaspoon cardamom
ground
1 tablespoon olive oil
salt and pepper

Combine all of the ingredients in a mixing bowl, and gently toss to mix Correct the seasonings, adding salt, lime juice, or sugar, to taste. The salsa should be a little sweet and a little sour. Best when served a couple hours after making. Cover and Refrigerate until serving time.

67   CHERRY TOMATO SALSA

2 pints cherry tomatoes
1 large shallot minced
1 large garlic clove minced
2 tablespoon minced fresh
coriander

1 tablespoon white wine
vinegar
2 Serrano chiles seeded and
minced
2 teaspoon fresh lime juice
1/4 teaspoon salt

In a food processor, coarsely chop the tomatoes, turning the machine on and off. Do not puree. In a medium bowl, combine the chopped tomatoes and their juices with the shallot, garlic, coriander, vinegar, chiles, lime juice and salt. Stir well. Cover with plastic wrap and set aside for at least 2 hours to blend the flavors.

68 CRAB SALSA

1/2 pound crab meat, fresh lump drained
1/2 cup lime juice, fresh
1 teaspoon tangerine rind grated
2/3 cup tangerine chopped
1/2 cup tomato peeled, seeded, chop

5 tablespoons red onion chopped
1 tablespoon cilantro chopped
1 tablespoon Jalapeño chopped
1/8 teaspoon salt

Combine ingredients and mix gently. Cover and chill. Serve with baked tortilla wedges or tortilla chips.

69 FOUR PEPPER SALSA

14 1/2 ounce Italian plum tomatoes drain
1 each medium. onion thinly sliced
1/2 cup coarsely chopped celery
1 can 4 ounce green chilies drained
1/3 cup chopped red bell pepper

1/3 cup chopped yellow bell pepper
1/3 cup chopped green bell pepper
1/4 cup olive oil
2 tablespoon red wine vinegar
1 teaspoon mustard seeds
1 teaspoon ground coriander
1 teaspoon salt
1 teaspoon pepper
1/4 cup chopped fresh cilantro

Combine first 13 ingredients in a processor. Finely chop using on/off turns. Transfer to bowl. Cover and chill at least 4 hours. Can be made two days ahead. Mix cilantro into salsa. Serve with chips.

70 ORANGE SALSA

2 large oranges peeled and diced

1 large tomato seeded and diced
1/3 cup red onion minced

1 teaspoon orange peel grated
1 teaspoon garlic minced
1 teaspoon ginger root minced

1/2 Jalapeño minced fine
1/4 teaspoon salt
1 tablespoon cilantro fresh

In a bowl combine all ingredients except the cilantro and chill, covered, until ready to serve. before serving, stir in the cilantro.

71 PINTO BEAN AND THREE CHILE SALSA

3/4 cup pinto beans, dried
1 teaspoon salt
3 arbol chiles, with seeds
3 pasilla chiles, seeded
2 Jalapeño chiles, for garnish
2 chipotle chiles
1/3 onion, diced

1/2 cup olive oil
2 garlic cloves, roasted
2 Roma tomatoes, blackened
3/4 cup dark beer
1 tablespoon peanut oil
1 teaspoon cider vinegar

Wash and drain beans, place in a large pot and cover with water. Cook until soft, about 1 1/2 hours, but it make take up to 2 hours. Drain and Transfer to a mixing bowl. Add the salt. Toast the arbol and pasilla chiles together. Re-hydrate all dried chiles in one cup of warm water. If using canned or fresh, omit this step. Drain and set aside. Roast and peel Jalapeño chiles, seed, dice and set aside. Heat olive oil and sauté the onion over medium-high heat until caramelized. Transfer to a blender along with the chiles (not the Jalapeño chiles), garlic, tomatoes, beer and puree. In a wok or large skillet, heat peanut oil until smoking hot and add the puree. Re-fry until reduced and thickened, this will take about 5 minutes. Transfer 3/4 of this re-fried mixture to a mixing bowl and add beans and cider vinegar. garnish with Jalapeño.

72 ROASTED PINEAPPLE CARROT SALSA

1 medium pineapple, ripe
1 teaspoon dark sesame oil
1/8 teaspoon red pepper ground
1 sweet onions sliced 1-inch thick
1 large Jalapeño seeded and halved
2 tablespoons red bell pepper diced

1/2 cup carrot chopped
2 tablespoons lime juice, fresh
2 tablespoons pineapple juice
1 tablespoon cider vinegar
1 teaspoon brown sugar
1 teaspoon ginger, fresh peeled and grated
1/8 teaspoon allspice ground

Preheat oven to 450. Cut both ends off of pineapple using a large sharp knife, and cut pineapple pulp from rind. Cut pineapple pulp lengthwise into quarters. Remove core from quarters; discard core. Reserve 2 quarters for another use. Combine sesame oil and ground red pepper, and brush over 2 pineapple quarters, onion slice, and sliced Jalapeño pepper. Place pineapple on a baking sheet, and bake at 450 for 15 minutes. Add onion, and bake an additional 10 minutes. Add sliced Jalapeño pepper, and bake an additional 10 minutes or until pineapple, onion, and Jalapeño are lightly browned. Remove from oven, and cool. Dice pineapple, onion, and Jalapeño, and combine with diced bell pepper in a medium bowl. cook carrot in boiling water 4 minutes or until crisp-tender. Combine carrot, lime juice, and remaining ingredients. Add to pineapple mixture; stir well.

73   SPICY NUT SALSA WITH BLUE CHEESE

3 tablespoons hazelnut oil or olive oil
4 teaspoons dry mustard
2 teaspoons ground allspice
1/2 cup hazelnuts coarsely chopped
1/2 cup pecan pieces

1/2 cup slivered almonds coarsely chopped
1 cup celery chopped
1 cup gorgonzola or blue cheese crumbled
2 tablespoons honey

Heat first 3 ingredients in heavy large skillet over medium heat. Add nuts and sauté until golden, about 7 minutes. Transfer to large bowl. Stir in celery, cheese and honey. Season with salt and pepper.

74   BLACKEYED PEA AND TOMATO SALSA

vegetable cooking spray
1 cup chopped onion
1/2 cup chopped lean Canadian-style bacon
2 clove garlic; minced
1/4 teaspoon ground cumin
1/4 teaspoon ground pepper

15 ounce black-eyed peas; (1 can) drained
14 1/2 ounce no-salt-added whole tomatoes chopped
1/3 cup minced fresh cilantro
1 tablespoon finely chopped fresh Jalapeño

Coat a large nonstick skillet with cooking spray; Place over medium heat until hot. Add onion and next 2 ingredients; sauté 5 minutes. Stir in cumin and next 3 ingredients; bring to a boil. Remove from heat; stir in remaining ingredients. Spoon into a bowl; cover and chill 1 to 8 hours. Serve at room temperature with Italian bread or no-oil tortilla chips.

75   CURRIED NECTARINE SALSA

1 teaspoon curry powder
2 cup nectarine; diced
1/2 cup red bell pepper; diced

1/4 cup red onion; diced
1/4 teaspoon salt

Place curry in a large skillet; cook over low heat 30 seconds or until fragrant, stirring occasionally. Remove skillet from heat; add nectarine and remaining ingredients, stirring until well blended. Serve warm or at room temperature.

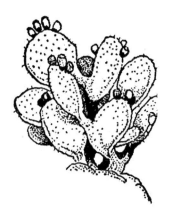

76 NAPALITO CACTUS SALSA

1 nopalito cactus; diced small
1/2 cup mixed peppers; sweet and hot, diced
1/2 cup mixed citrus supremes; chopped (orange/grapefruit)
1/2 cup diced tomatoes
1 tablespoon chives; sliced
3 tablespoon cilantro; chopped
2 tablespoon onion; diced
juice of 2 limes
2 tablespoon olive oil(substitute 1 teaspoon oil; and 1 teaspoon broth or juice)
salt and pepper
1/2 cup tequila

77 STRAWBERRY KIWI SALSA

2 strawberry kiwi tea bags
1/4 cup apple cider vinegar
4 tablespoon light soy sauce
1 teaspoon minced garlic
1 1/2 teaspoon sugar
3 kiwi fruit; peeled and diced
1/2 cup strawberries; diced
1/4 cup fresh cilantro; chopped

To prepare the salsa, steep the tea bags in the vinegar for 15 minutes. Remove the bags, squeezing out the excess liquid, and discard the bags. Add the soy sauce, garlic, sugar, kiwis, cilantro, and strawberries and toss.

78 JICAMA VIDALIA SALSA

1 jicama (1 pound)
1 large vidalia onion
2 small carrots
3 cloves garlic
1/4 cup white vinegar
2 fresh Jalapeños
5 dried Anchos
2 dried Habañeros
cilantro
1 dash salt

Peel the jicama, onion, and carrot, dice. Throw everything in the blender and grind to your liking. You may need to add just a bit more vinegar (or for an extra kick a shot or two of tequila) if the mixture is too dry. let stand or refrigerate for at least 2 hours to let everything meld. Use creatively. Of course, use the chiles of your preference, and in your preferred quantities. The idea is to blend a nice deep burn with a sweet aftertaste (from the sweet onion and jicama).

79 CORN AND GREENS SALSA

3 ears corn
1/4 cup water
3 tablespoon apple cider
vinegar
8 ounce mixed watercress
mustard greens and arugula;
roughly julienned

2 red Thai or Serrano chiles
thinly sliced
1/4 teaspoon salt
1/2 teaspoon freshly ground
pepper

Cut the corn kernels from the cobs with a sharp knife. Place in a sauté pan with the water and cook for 2-3 minutes on medium heat until tender and the water has evaporated. Put in mixing bowl. Heat the vinegar in a large pan or skillet and wilt the greens over medium head for 30 sec. Add to the mixing bowl with the chiles, salt and pepper, and thoroughly combine.

80 ORANGE AND LEMON SALSA

1 medium navel orange
1 large lemon
2 tablespoon finely chopped
fresh rosemary

one lemon; (about 2
tablespoon) juice of
1 tablespoon sucanat

Peel zest from the orange and lemon, leaving the white pith intact on the fruit. Slice half the zest into very thin strips, about 1/16 inch thick. Discard remaining zest or save for another use. Cut the peeled orange and lemon, including pith, into quarters. Put fruit into food processor or blender and coarsely chop. Pour fruit into a small saucepan and stir in rosemary, juice, and sucanat. Cook over medium heat for 2 or 3 minutes. Remove from heat, stir in zest, and let cool. Spoon into a sterilized jar and refrigerate. The salsa will keep for 7to 10 days.

81 CORN AND SQUASH SALSA

2 tablespoon diced onion
1/4 cup water
2 ears corn
1 1/2 cup yellow squash;
diced to size of corn kernels
2 large sprigs fresh marjoram
5 Roma tomatoes; oven
roasted and diced or red bell

peppers; roasted, skinned and diced

1 teaspoon minced fresh marjoram
1/3 teaspoon salt

Sauté onion in water over low heat, covered for 10 minutes. Cut the corn kernels from the cobs with a sharp knife. Add to sauté pan along with squash and sprigs of marjoram. Cook for 5 minutes., until vegetables are soft and water has evaporated. Discard marjoram. Transfer to bowl. Add tomatoes or peppers, marjoram, and salt and stir well. Chill before serving.

82 ROSEMARY ONION SALSA

2 teaspoon olive oil
5 cup red onion; slivered
1 tablespoon sugar
2 tablespoon red wine vinegar

1 1/2 teaspoon fresh rosemary; use less if dried
1/4 teaspoon salt
1/4 teaspoon pepper

Heat oil in a large nonstick skillet over medium high heat. Add onion. Sauté for 7 minutes or until lightly browned. Add sugar, red wine vinegar and remaining ingredients; reduce heat to medium, and sauté for an additional five minutes. Serve warm or at room temperature.

83 LIME ORANGE SALSA

4 navel oranges
1 small red onion; finely chopped
1/4 cup fresh lime juice
1/4 cup chopped fresh cilantro

1 tablespoon chipotle peppers; minced
1 clove garlic; minced
salt and ground black pepper to taste

With a sharp knife, Remove skin and white pith from oranges and discard. Working over a medium-sized bowl to catch the juice, cut the orange segments from their surrounding membrane, letting the segments fall into the bowl. Add onions, lime juice, cilantro, chipotle peppers and garlic. Stir to combine. Season with salt and pepper. (salsa can be made ahead and stored, covered, in the refrigerator for up to 8 hours.)

84 WATERMELON STRAWBERRY MINT SALSA

1 cup watermelon; diced and seeded
3/4 cup strawberries; diced
1/4 cup red onion; diced
2 tablespoon Jalapeño; diced
2 tablespoon fresh mint leaves; finely chopped
2 tablespoon olive oil

1 tablespoon lime juice   1 teaspoon sugar

85 APPLE BERRY SALSA

2 medium granny smith
apples peel/core/chop
1 cup strawberries hulled and
sliced
1 kiwi peeled and chopped
1 small orange

2 tablespoon brown sugar
2 tablespoon apple jelly
zest orange (about 2
tablespoon.)
1/4 cup orange juice

86 GREEN CHILI SALSA WITH CUMIN AND CARDAMOM

4 oz fresh green chilies
roughly chopped
4 large garlic cloves peeled
and minced
1/2 cup roughly chopped
parsley

1/2 cup roughly chopped
cilantro
fresh lemon juice
1 teaspoon black pepper
1 teaspoon ground cumin
1/4 teaspoon ground
cardamom

Puree the chilies with the garlic and fresh herbs in a small food processor. Add a little lemon juice or water to help blend the mixture, if necessary, then add the spices and blend again. Dilute with lemon juice, as needed. Do not remove the seeds and veins from the chilies before you chop them for hotter flavor.

87 GUAJILLO SALSA

1/2 pound dried Guajillo
chiles
3 cup water
5 large cloves roasted garlic
1 teaspoon ground cumin
1 teaspoon salt

1/2 pound Roma tomatoes
2 teaspoon toasted pumpkin
seeds
1/2 cup cider vinegar
1 teaspoon Mexican oregano
roasted and ground

Stem and seed the chiles, then place them in a skillet, on a comal, or in a 250 degree oven and dry-roast them for 3 or 4 minutes. Shake them once or twice and be careful not to scorch them or else they will taste bitter; this in turn will make sauce taste bitter. The chiles should then be added to water that has been heated. Temperature must be below boiling point, otherwise the chiles will lose flavor. Use just enough water to cover the chiles and press them down with a lid. Allow them to sit for 20 minutes or until they are soft. At this point, you should taste the water to see if it is bitter, discarding it if it is. The chiles can then be used as directed in the recipe.

Puree the chiles with the remaining ingredients. To use as a sauce, heat 2 tablespoons peanut oil or lard in a high-sided pan and refry the sauce at a sizzle for 3 to 5 minutes, stirring continuously. Add water if necessary.

88 PEACH AND APRICOT SALSA

3 cup peaches, peeled and chopped
3 cup apricots, chopped
2 cup shiro plums, sliced
2 tablespoon lemon juice
6 cup sugar
1 teaspoon butter

In a Dutch oven, combine 2 cup each of the peaches and apricots with the remaining ingredients excepting the butter. Mash enough to break the fruit. Stir in the remaining peaches and apricots. Add butter bring to a slow boil, stirring. boil, continuing to stir frequently, for 20 minutes or until setting point is reached.

89 POMEGRANATE BLACK BEAN SALSA

1 chile, Poblano roasted, peeled, stemmed seeded and diced
2 cup beans, black, cooked rinsed
2 tablespoon juice, pomegranate, fresh
1/4 cup bell peppers, red stemmed, seeded, diced
1/4 cup bell peppers, yellow stemmed, seeded, diced
2 garlic cloves; roasted peeled, chopped
1 onion, white roasted and chopped
1 tablespoon chiles chipotle en adobo (canned)
1 tablespoon cilantro, fresh, chopped
1/4 teaspoon cumin seed, toasted ground
salt

Combine all ingredients in plastic or glass bowl; toss briefly in a sauté pan over medium heat; salt to taste.

90 ORANGE HABAÑERO SALSA

1 Habañero
2 carrots
3 cloves garlic
1/4 cup water
2 tablespoon chopped white onion
1 teaspoon salt
3 tablespoon freshly squeezed lemon juice
1/4 cup ginger pickle juice
1 teaspoon sugar
1/2 orange zested

Steam carrots and garlic with water until soft in the microwave. Put everything in the blender and puree till smooth. Adjust flavors.

91 VERY BERRY SALSA

1 pint blueberries
1 pint strawberries
¼ cup sugar
3 teaspoon minced sweet onion

1 teaspoon blueberry or
raspberry vinegar or lemon
juice
1 teaspoon freshly ground
black pepper

hot pepper sauce to taste
¼ cup sliced or slivered
almonds toasted

Rinse the blueberries and strawberries, then dry on paper towels.
Pick over the berries. Hull the strawberries and cut into quarters. In a
bowl combine the blueberries, strawberries, sugar, onion, vinegar,
pepper and hot pepper sauce. Mix well and refrigerate for at least one
hour. Just before serving, stir in the almonds. Serve over fruit sorbet
or as a condiment with poultry or pork.

92 ROASTED CORN RED ONION AND GARLIC SALSA

4 ears fresh corn, husked
2 tablespoon unsalted butter,
melted
5 ripe tomatoes, seeded and
cut into 1/4-inch dice
1/2 small red onion, peeled
and finely chopped
1 small Jalapeño pepper,
finely chopped, or to taste

1 small clove garlic, peeled
and finely chopped
1/2 cup cilantro leaves,
coarsely chopped
3 tablespoon fresh lime juice,
plus more to taste
salt and freshly ground pepper

Brush corn with melted butter and place on a medium-hot grill or
under a broiler, turning often, until about half the kernels are brown,
15 to 20 minutes. Remove corn from heat and let cool. Using a sharp
knife, cut kernels from cobs. Combine corn, tomatoes, onion,
Jalapeño, garlic, and cilantro in a medium bowl. Season to taste with
time juice, salt, and pepper.

93 ROASTED WHITE CORN SALSA

2 cup sweet white corn
1/4 cup olive oil
salt and freshly ground pepper
1/3 cup red bell pepper finely
diced
2/3 cup red onion finely diced

1 teaspoon Serrano chile
minced seeded
1 tablespoon cherry vinegar
1 teaspoon fresh lemon juice
1 teaspoon honey

Toss corn with oil and lightly season with salt and pepper. Spread out
in a single layer on a baking sheet and roast in a preheated oven at
425 until very lightly browned. Cool and add to a bowl with rest of
ingredients. Cover and store refrigerated for up to 5 days.

1 cup dried black beans,
soaked overnight and drained
4 cup water
1 small onion
1 small carrot, chopped
1/2 cup green peppers,
chopped
1 chili, Jalapeño or Serrano
seeded and coarsely chopped
2 garlic cloves, chopped
1 bay leaf
1 teaspoon soy sauce, low-
sodium
1/2 teaspoon cumin, ground
1/4 teaspoon red pepper
flakes, crushed
saffron rice
2 1/4 cup vegetable stock
saffron threads, pinch
1/3 cup onions, chopped
finely

1 teaspoon olive oil
1 garlic clove, minced
1/2 teaspoon turmeric
1 1/2 cup rice, long-grain,
white
chunky tomato salsa
2 cup tomatoes, diced
1/2 avocado, large, diced
1/2 cup red onions
1/2 cup cucumbers, diced
2 tablespoon coriander, fresh,
minced
1 tablespoon lime juice
1 teaspoon olive oil
1 teaspoon chili peppers,
minced
garnishes
soy yogurt, optional
coriander leaves, garnish

To make the beans: in a 3 quart saucepan, combine the beans, water,
onion, carrot, green peppers, chili pepper, garlic, bay leaf, soy sauce,
cumin and pepper flakes. Bring to a boil over medium-high heat,
stirring occasionally. Reduce the heat to medium and simmer,
uncovered, for about 2-1/2 hours, or until the beans are tender and
almost all the liquid has been absorbed. Discard the bay leaf and set
aside the bean mixture(may be made up to 2 days ahead; reheat
before serving). To make the rice: in a 1 quart saucepan, bring 1/4 of
the stock to a boil. Add the saffron. cover, remove from the heat and
let stand for 5 minutes. In a 2 quart saucepan over low heat, sauté the
onions in the oil until tender, about 5 minutes. Add the garlic and
sauté for 1 minute. stir in the turmeric, then the rice. Add the
remaining 2 cup stock and the saffron mixture. Bring to a boil over
high heat, then reduce the heat to low, cover the pan and simmer for
15 minutes, or until the rice is tender and all the liquid has been
absorbed. Lightly coat 4 (8 ounce) custard cups with no-stick spray or
olive oil. Spoon about 3/4 cup of the warm rice into each cup,
pressing it into the bottom and up the sides. Add about 1/2 cup of the
beans to each cup. Top with more rice to cover the t
it around the edges. If not serving the timbales imm
each cup tightly with a piece of foil. Set the cups on
and keep warm at 300(for up to 30 minutes). To mal
medium bowl, combine the tomatoes, avocado, onio

coriander, lime juice, oil and peppers. If not serving immediately, cover and refrigerate. To serve: Remove the foil from the timbale. Invert each cup onto a dinner plate. Top with the salsa and soy yogurt. garnish with the coriander.

95 SWEET AND MILD SALSA

4 pound tomatoes, peeled, chopped
1 each large red bell pepper
1 each large green bell pepper
4 each Jalapeño peppers

1 each large yellow onion
1 tablespoon garlic powder
1 teaspoon ground red pepper
1 small bunch parsley

Peel the tomatoes and chop. Cut and seed all the peppers. Place tomatoes in food processor and blend well, (should still be slightly lumpy). Place in large pot and bring to a boil. Place red pepper in food processor and chop until very fine. Add to tomatoes. process onion and add to mix in pot. Process remaining ingredients and stir into tomato mix. Cook, to reduce liquid, about 15 to 20 minutes at a slow boil. Drain in strainer and place in jars. Add enough liquid just to make juicy.

96 SALSA DE PIMENTOS

2 red bell peppers, roasted peeled,, cut in chunks
4 hard cooked egg yolks
1 cup half and half
1 teaspoon paprika
2 tablespoon olive oil
1 tablespoon Anchovy paste

1/2 teaspoon sea salt
1/4 teaspoon freshly ground black pepper
3 tablespoon lemon juice
dash of Tabasco
20 stuffed olives thinly sliced

In a blender, combine the red peppers, egg yolks, half and half, paprika, oil, Anchovy paste, salt, and pepper. Blend until smooth. Pour into a bowl and add the lemon juice, Tabasco, and olives.

97 SALSA DE PINON (PESTO)

3/4 cup pine nuts, toasted and cooled
3 hard cooked egg yolks
2 tablespoon caper juice
2 tablespoon capers

1 cup half and half
sea salt,, to taste
freshly ground black pepper, to taste

In a blender, combine the pine nuts, egg yolks, caper juice, capers, and half and half. blend until smooth. season with salt and pepper.

98 SALSA QUEMADA EL TORITO

nound firm, just-ripe
   ·toes

4 each scallions, include tops
4 each green Serrano chiles

1/2 each medium onion, peeled
2 each cloves garlic, minced
1 each juice of 2 fresh limes
1/2 each bunch of cilantro, chopped
1 teaspoon dried oregano
1/4 teaspoon ground white pepper
1 each salt to taste
2 ounce water
2 pound firm, just-ripe tomatoes
4 each scallions, including green tops

4 each green Serrano chiles
1 each half medium onion, peeled
2 each cloves garlic, peeled and minced
1 each juice of 2 fresh limes
1 each half a bunch of cilantro coarsely chopped
1 teaspoon dried oregano
1/4 teaspoon ground white pepper
1 each salt to taste
2 ounce water

Build a charcoal fire, then scatter pre soaked mesquite chips over the coals. Carefully grill tomatoes, scallions and chiles over glowing coals, turning frequently, until skin is charred. Remove from grill and leave skin on vegetables. Remove stems from tomatoes and chiles. Cut tomatoes, scallions, chiles and onion into chunks. Place in food processor or blender, then pulse on-off until mixture is coarse. Mix in remaining ingredients. Chill at least 2 hours before serving.

99 LARGE PARILLA GREEN CHILE SALSA

1 clove garlic
1 thick slice white onion
1 Roma (plum) tomato
1 tomatillo
3 Poblano chilies
1/2 cup water

1 tablespoon fresh cilantro roughly chopped
1/8 teaspoon kosher salt
1/4 teaspoon cumin toasted and ground

Pan roast garlic until brown and soft, then peel. Pan roast onion until brown and soft, then roughly chop. Pan roast tomato until blistered, deeply browned, and soft. Pan roast tomatillo until blistered, browned, and soft. Pan roast Poblano chilies until dark brown, then remove seed cores. Place the garlic, onion, tomato, tomatillo, and chilies in a food processor and pulse briefly until finely chopped. Add the water, cilantro, salt and cumin and process again until blended. Keeps, tightly covered, about 3 days in the refrigerator.

100   SWEET SALSA

1 clove garlic diced
1 tablespoon ginger root diced
1/2 medium Spanish onion diced

1 splash rose's lime juice
1 tangerine peeled and diced
1/2 pear cored and diced
4 strips dry mango diced

3 sprigs watercress finely
chopped
2 tablespoon dried mint
crumbled

1 tablespoon olive oil
salt and pepper

In a medium bowl mix together the garlic, ginger and onion with the
lime juice. Stir in remaining ingredients and season to taste. Serve
with chips, seafood and vegetables.

101   MINT AND CARAMELIZED SHALLOT SALSA

10 shallots; peeled and thinly
sliced
1 tablespoon fresh ginger;
grated
1/4 cup fresh mint; minced
1/2 cup minced fresh
pineapple
2 tablespoon pineapple juice

1 teaspoon minced Thai red
chilies or 1 1/2 teaspoon
minced red Serranos
3/4 teaspoon sugar
1 teaspoon soy sauce
2 tablespoon unseasoned rice
wine vinegar

Sauté shallots in water until browned, about 10 minutes. Cool. Mix
with the remaining ingredients.

102   WHITE WINE VINEGER AND RED PEPPER SALSA

2 large red bell peppers;
chopped
1 small round onion; chopped
2 cloves garlic; minced
1/4 cup water
1/2 tablespoon white wine
vinegar

1/8 teaspoon crushed red
pepper
1/8 teaspoon white pepper
2 dash Tabasco sauce
1 tablespoon horseradish

Place peppers, onion and garlic in a sauce pan with the water. cover
and cook over low heat until peppers are very soft, about 15 minutes.
Transfer to a food processor or blender and process until smooth.
return to sauce pan. Add remaining ingredients. heat over low heat for
5 minutes to blend flavors, stirring occasionally.

103 ROASTED CORN AND WILD MUSHROOM SALSA

4 ears fresh corn
1/3 cup cleaned and diced
fresh wild mushrooms
1/4 cup sun-dried tomatoes
2 Poblano chilies; roasted,
peeled, seeded and diced

2 teaspoon minced fresh
marjoram
1 clove roasted garlic; minced
1 teaspoon adobo sauce
1 teaspoon fresh lime juice
1/2 teaspoon sherry vinegar
1/2 teaspoon salt

Cut the corn kernels from the cobs with a sharp knife. Heat a large
pan or skillet over high heat until almost smoking. Place no more than

2 layers of the corn kernels in the pan at a time and dry-roast for 4-5 minutes until smoky and dark (stirring continuously). Sauté the mushrooms for 10 minutes. Mix with the corn and add the remaining ingredients.

104 TOMATO AND BLACK OLIVE SALSA

4 ripe tomatoes (chopped, seeded, and drained)
1 bunch green onions
1 can black olives (pitted and sliced)

1 teaspoon dry cilantro
1 can mild green chilies
1 clove garlic (minced)
salt (to taste)

Chop the onions and chilies. Mix all the ingredients together. Prepare salsa shortly before serving and let sit at room temperature for a little while. Serve with taco chips.

105 HABANARO SUICIDE SALSA

12 ripe Habañero peppers
12 fresh Jalapeño peppers
1/2 cup dried Tabasco chilies
4 hot banana peppers
1 sweet green pepper
1 sweet red pepper
1 medium cooking onion

2 bulbs garlic
6 tablespoon. salt
2 tablespoon. black pepper corns, coarsely ground
4 tablespoon. sugar
6 cups water

Put on heavy rubber gloves! core and Remove seeds from the sweet peppers. Peel the onion and garlic. Coarsely chop the onion, garlic, and all the peppers, both how and sweet. Place all the ingredients in a large saucepan. Cover and simmer for at least an hour, adding small amounts of water and stirring as needed as the water level decreases. Remove it from the heat and place the contents in the bowl of a food processor. Puree it until smooth. Push the contents through a strainer with the back of a wooden spoon (the mixture will be thick). Pour it into sterilized bottles when cool and place on the lids. Store it in the refrigerator.

106 MEXICAN CAVIAR SALSA

2 large tomatoes, finely chopped
5 green onions, chopped
3 tablespoon. olive oil
3 1/2 tablespoon. tarragon vinegar

1 (4 ounce) can chopped green chile peppers
1 (2 1/4 ounce) can chopped black olives
1 teaspoon garlic salt
1 teaspoon salt

Mix all the ingredients together thoroughly in a large glass bowl. Cover and refrigerate for at least 6 hours before serving.

107 LUSTY EGGPLANT SALSA

3 pound eggplants
2 tablespoon salt
1/3 cup extra virgin olive oil
1 small onion, thinly sliced
1 small red bell pepper, julienned
6 garlic cloves, thinly sliced

1 teaspoon oregano leaves or
1 teaspoon dried oregano
1 teaspoon capers, drained
1/2 teaspoon dried hot red pepper flakes
3 cup white wine vinegar
2 tablespoon sugar

Peel the eggplant and cut into 1/8 inch julienne strips about 2 inches long. Place the eggplant in a colander, add the salt and toss well. Cover the colander, Place over a large bowl, and let stand for 1 hour. Combine the oil, onion, pepper and garlic in a large, heavy, non-reactive Dutch oven or deep skillet, Place over medium heat, and sauté the mixture for 5 minutes. Add the eggplant and sauté until golden on all sides, for about 5 minutes. Stir in the oregano, capers, and hot pepper flakes.. Remove the pan from the heat and divide the eggplant mixture among 6 sterilized half-pint jars. Return the Dutch oven to the stove and add the vinegar and sugar. turn the heat up to high and bring the mixture to a boil. Reduce the heat and simmer for 5 minutes. Remove the pan from the heat and spoon the liquid mixture equally into the 6 eggplant jars, leaving a 1/4 inch head space in each jar. Seal the jars and process in a boiling water bath for 15 minutes. Let cool and store in a cool, dark Place for 2 to 3 weeks before using.

108 CRANAPPLE SALSA

1 apple
1 navel orange; peeled
2 cup fresh or frozen cranberries

1/2 teaspoon ground coriander;
2 packet equal sweetener (4 teaspoons)

Shred the apple in a food processor or with a hand grater. Quarter the orange and Combine with the cranberries in a food processor or food grinder. Process until coarsely chopped. Blend the apples, cranberry mixture, coriander, and sweetener together. Cover and refrigerate until ready to serve.

109 ZUCCHINI SALSA

2 cup zucchini; shredded
2 tablespoon lime juice
1/4 teaspoon pepper
1/4 cup fresh cilantro; snipped

2 tablespoon vegetable or olive oil
1/4 teaspoon sugar

Mix all ingredients in glass or plastic bowl. Refrigerate at least 1 hour.

110 RADISH AND CILANTRO SALSA

2 cup radishes; thinly sliced
3 tablespoon orange juice
2 tablespoon fresh cilantro;
fine snipped
1/4 teaspoon salt

1/2 cup onion; chopped, 1
medium
2 tablespoon lime juice
2 tablespoon vegetable oil
1/8 teaspoon pepper; freshly
ground

Mix all ingredients in glass or plastic bowl. Refrigerate at least 1 hour

111 CRANBERRY ONION SALSA

1/4 cup chopped onion
1 small clove garlic minced
1 cup cranberries

3 tablespoon sugar
1 tablespoon water
1 teaspoon cider vinegar

Coat a small saucepan with cooking spray; Place over medium-high
heat until hot. Add onion and garlic. Sauté until tender. Add
cranberries, sugar and 1 teaspoon. water. bring to a boil; cook 3 to 5
minutes or until mixture is thickened. Stir in vinegar. Store in an
airtight container and Refrigerate. Serve at room temperature.

112 CHERRY HONEY SALSA

20 ounce pitted cherries with
juice (1 can)
1/2 cup raisins
1/2 cup honey
1/4 cup cider vinegar
1/4 cup brown sugar, firmly
packed

1/2 teaspoon ground
cinnamon
1/8 teaspoon ground cloves
1/2 cup pecans, chopped
(medium)coarse
1 tablespoon cornstarch
1 tablespoon cold water

In a 2-quart saucepan, combine all the ingredients through the clove
listing. cook slowly, uncovered, for 30 minutes. Stir in the pecans.
Combine the cornstarch and cold water, blending well, and gradually
stir into the cherry mixture. Cook, stirring constantly, until the
mixture thickens. use this with light meats such as duck, pork, or
chicken.

113 TURKEY BREAST ORANGE BLACKBERRY SALSA

1 medium size orange, seeded
and coarsely chopped
1/3 cup plus 2 teaspoon.
frozen orange juice
concentrate thawed and
undiluted and divided

1/4 cup firmly packed brown
sugar
2 tablespoon cornstarch
one (16 ounce) package
frozen unsweetened
blackberries, thawed and
drained

1/4 cup water
one (6 pound) turkey breast
skinned
12 leaf lettuce leaves

2 medium size oranges cut
into 1/4 inch slices
2 1/2 tablespoon salsa.

With knife blade in processor, Add chopped orange. Process for 1 1/2
minutes. or until finely chopped. Place chopped orange in a medium
non- aluminum saucepan. Add 2 teaspoon. orange juice concentrate,
brown sugar, cornstarch and thawed blackberries; stirring gently.
Place over medium-low heat and cook for 7 minutes or until mixture
thickens, stirring constantly. Place in a medium bowl; cover and chill.
Combine remaining 1/3 cup orange juice concentrate and 1/4 cup
water. Set aside. Place turkey breast on a rack covered with cooking
spray and place rack in a shallow roasting pan. Insert meat
thermometer into meaty portion, making sure it does not touch the
bone. Baste turkey breast with orange juice mixture. Cover and bake
at 325 for about 1 hour. Uncover and bake turkey breast for an
additional 1 hour or until meat thermometer registers 170
temperature., basting frequently with orange juice mixture. Place
turkey breast on a lettuce lined serving platter; cover loosely with foil
and let stand for about 15 minutes. before slicing. Arrange orange
slices around turkey slices and Serve salsa with turkey.

114 HARVEST GOLD SALSA

1 1/2 cup whole kernel corn
2/3 cup chopped tomato
1/2 cup chopped green pepper
1/4 cup finely chopped green
onions
2 tablespoon brown sugar

1/2 Jalapeño pepper, seeded
and minced
1/4 cup dilled vinegar
1/4 teaspoon salt
1/4 cup minced fresh dill

Combine first 7 ingredients in a heavy, non-aluminum saucepan;
bring to a boil. Reduce heat to medium low and simmer, uncovered
for 20-25 minutes. or until liquid has evaporated, stirring frequently.
Remove from heat; stir in salt. Let it cool for 5 minutes. Stir in dill.
Spoon it into a serving bowl. Let it cool to room temperature.

115 CUCUMBER PEPPER SALSA

1 lemon grass stalk
1/2 cup rice vinegar
1/4 cup sugar
1/2 teaspoon red pepper flakes
2 cucumber, medium
1 banana pepper;
devein/minced

1 Serrano, red;
deveined/minced
2 teaspoon cilantro; minced
2 teaspoon basil, fresh;
minced
2 teaspoon mint, fresh;
minced

1/3 cup lime juice   1 pepper, white
1 salt

Bring lemon grass, vinegar, sugar, red pepper flakes and 1/2 cup water to boil in a saucepan; simmer until reduced to 1/2 cup. Strain mixture into a bowl and cool slightly; discard solids. Stir in all other sauce ingredients. Sprinkle scallops with 1/2 teaspoon salt and 1/4 teaspoon white pepper. Heat one tablespoon oil in a wok or non-stick skillet. Working in batches to avoid overcrowding, and adding remaining oil as needed, sauté scallops, turning once, until seared. Spoon a portion of salsa onto each plate. Arrange a portion of scallops over the salsa. Serve immediately.

116 GARDEN SALSA

2 each cucumbers
12 medium sized onions
4 green peppers
2 medium-sized carrots
6 cup granulated sugar

4 cup apple cider vinegar
12 whole cloves
1 tablespoon mustard seed
2 tablespoon turmeric

Grind cucumbers, onions, peppers and carrots together until a fine pasties made. Stir in salt and Let set overnight. Drain well. Mix in remaining ingredients. Place cloves and mustard seed in cloth bags. Bring to a boil and simmer gently for 30 minutes. Remove bag of spices. Spoon into the hot sterilized jars and seal.

117 SOUTHWEST SALSA

1 cup tomatillo, chopped
3/4 cup tomato, seeded and chopped
3/4 cup green bell pepper, diced
3/4 cup yellow bell pepper, diced

1/4 cup pine nuts, toasted
2 cloves garlic, fine chopped
1 tablespoon fresh sage leaves, snipped
1 tablespoon lemon juice
1/4 teaspoon salt

Mix all ingredients. Cover and refrigerate at least for 1 hour.

118 TOMATO SALSA WITH MOROCCAN LEMONS

2 small green bell peppers
1 can tomatoes (28 ounce)
1 garlic clove, pressed/minced
2 tablespoon olive oil

3/4 teaspoon ground cumin
1/4 teaspoon paprika
1/4 teaspoon pepper
3 Moroccan preserved lemons

Place bell peppers in a 9-10 inch wide pan; Broil 4 inch from heat, turning as needed, until charred on all sides, for 15-20 minutes. Cool. Remove peel, stems, and seeds. Chop peppers. Drain tomatoes, reserving juice for another use. Coarsely chop tomatoes; Drain well. In a bowl, mix bell peppers, tomatoes, garlic, oil, cumin, paprika, and pepper. Add preserved lemon to taste. Serve, or cover and chill up to a day.

119   RAISIN CRANBERRY SALSA

1 large tart cooking apple, coarsely chopped
8 ounce whole cranberry sauce
1/2 cup seedless golden raisins

2 tablespoon chopped dried apricots
1 medium lemon, grated peel and juice
1/4 teaspoon salt
1/4 teaspoon ground cinnamon

Combine all of the ingredients in a large saucepan. gradually heat to boiling, stirring often. Simmer for 5 minutes then cool to room temperature. Cover and Refrigerate. Serve chilled.

120   CINNAMON MUSTARD SEED TOMATO SALSA

18 each firm ripe tomatoes
1 stalk celery
4 medium. onions
2 sweet green peppers
2 sweet red peppers
1/3 cup salt
2 1/4 cup granulated sugar

1/2 teaspoon ground cloves
2 teaspoon cinnamon
1/2 teaspoon black pepper
2 tablespoon mustard seed, tied in bag
1 1/2 cup apple cider vinegar

Peel tomatoes, then chop into small pieces. chop celery, onions, and peppers into fine pieces. Mix together the vegetables and salt. Place in refrigerator overnight. Drain thoroughly in the morning. Combine sugar, spices and vinegar, making sure the sugar is dissolved, in a large saucepan. bring to a boil and simmer 3 minutes. Add vegetables and return to a boil. simmer for 10 more minutes, stirring occasionally. Remove cheesecloth bag holding mustard seeds. spoon into hot sterilized jars and seal.

121   DATE AND CRANBERRY SALSA

1/2 pound fresh cranberries
12 medium dates; coarsely chopped
1/2 lemon; seeded and diced

1/3 cup sugar
1 tablespoon cider vinegar
1 pinch cayenne pepper

The sweetness of the dates contrasts nicely with the tart cranberries giving this dish a north African holiday twist. Put cranberries, dates and lemon in a food processor and process until well combined but not totally smooth. Combine sugar, vinegar and cayenne. Add to mixture and pulse a few times. Chill an hour before serving.

122 BABY CORN SALSA

2 tablespoon oriental sesame oil

1 tablespoon minced fresh ginger

1 tablespoon minced shallot

1/2 teaspoon hot red chilies, crushed, dried

1/2 teaspoon ground coriander

1/2 cup rice vinegar

1/3 cup soy sauce

2 tablespoon oyster sauce

Pour oil into a 10-12 inch frying pan. Place over medium-high heat until oil just starts to smoke, for about 2 minutes. All at once, add ginger, shallot, chilies, and coriander. Stir for 30 seconds. at once, add rice vinegar, soy sauce, and oyster sauce. Boil, uncovered, over high heat until sauce is reduced to 1 cup, for about 1 minute.

123 BEET CABBAGE SALSA

10 beets, chopped

1 cup chopped onions

2 cup chopped cabbage

1 cup red sweet pepper

1 stalk celery, chopped

1/2 cup sugar

1 cup chopped cauliflower

3 tablespoon mustard seed

1 tablespoon celery seed

2 to 2 1/4 cups vinegar

Combine ingredients. Heat to boiling. Cook slowly, until vegetables are tender.

124 CRANBERRY CHERRY SALSA

1 cup cherries, canned or fresh

1 1/2 cup cranberries

2 cup brown sugar

1 1/2 cup raisins

1/2 teaspoon cinnamon

1/2 teaspoon cloves

1 orange

1 lemon

1/2 cup vinegar

1/2 stick cinnamon

1/2 teaspoon nutmeg

Pit cherries. wash cranberries. Remove stems. wash orange and lemon. cut in small pieces. Remove seeds. Combine ingredients. Mix thoroughly. cook slowly, stirring frequently, until thick..

125 GOOSEBERRY SALSA

5 cup gooseberries

1 cup brown sugar

1 1/2 cup raisins

1 onion, peeled and sliced

3 tablespoon salt

1/4 teaspoon cayenne pepper

1 teaspoon mustard

1 teaspoon ginger

1 teaspoon turmeric

1 quart vinegar

Chop gooseberries, raisins, and onion. Add other ingredients. heat slowly to boiling. simmer for 3/4 hour. Stir frequently. Rub through coarse sieve. Reheat.

126 GREEN OLIVE SALSA

1/4 cup pitted, cured green olives
1 teaspoon minced garlic
1/2 medium. red onion, diced small
1/4 cup chopped fresh parsley

1/4 cup olive oil, (extra virgin. preferred)
1/4 cup fresh lemon juice
salt and freshly ground black pepper

In a medium-size bowl or jar, combine all ingredients except salt and pepper. Mix well, then add salt and pepper to taste. cover and Refrigerate. Will keep for about 4 days.

127 JEWELED SALSA

1 can un-drained sauerkraut
2 cup celery, chopped
1 cup chopped olive w/pimento

1/2 cup honey
green pepper, chopped
carrot, grated
dill or garlic

Combine all ingredients. Allow to blend for 8 to 10 hours. Chill.

128 APPLE ONION PLUM SALSA

2 pound apples
4 medium onions
1 quart vinegar
2 tablespoon grated ginger root
2 tablespoon cloves

6 pound plums, pitted
1 teaspoon garlic salt
2 tablespoon salt
1/2 teaspoon red pepper
2 pound brown sugar

Pare and core apples. chop apples, onions, and plums. Combine all ingredients. cook slowly, stirring frequently, until thick.

129 SPICY PEAR SALSA

3 large firm ripe pears
5 whole cloves
3 thick lemon slices

1/4 teaspoon cinnamon
1/4 cup granulated sugar
1/8 teaspoon salt

Pare, halve, and core pears; slice 1/2 inch thick. Add lemon slices and combine remaining ingredients; simmer, covered, for 15 to 25 minutes.; or until tender. Cool; Refrigerate. Serve with poultry, or as dessert. makes 4 servings.

130 STRAWBERRY SALSA

2 tablespoon balsamic vinegar
2 tablespoon orange juice
1 tablespoon Dijon mustard

1 tablespoon honey
1/2 teaspoon grated orange peel

1/2 teaspoon red pepper flakes
2 cup strawberries, sliced
3 tablespoon raisins

3 tablespoon walnuts,
chopped

Combine first 6 ingredients and whisk to blend thoroughly. Add
remaining ingredients and toss. Serve this chutney style
accompaniment with grilled fish or chicken.

131 POMEGRANATE EGGPLANT SALSA

1/3 cup olive oil
1 medium eggplant; diced
medium
1 medium red onion; diced
small
2 tablespoon minced garlic
1 cup tomato juice

1/3 cup pomegranate
molasses
salt and pepper; to taste
1/4 cup roughly chopped fresh
mint
1 each pomegranate; seeds of

In a large sauté pan, heat oil over high heat until hot but not smoking.
Add eggplant and cook, stirring, until well seared and quite soft, for
about 5 to 7 minutes. Reduce heat to medium, Add onion and cook,
stirring, for 2 to 3 minutes. Add garlic and cook, stirring, for 1
minute. Add tomato juice and pomegranate molasses, bring just to a
boil, reduce heat to low and simmer, stirring occasionally, for 5
minutes. Remove from heat, season with salt and pepper, stir in the
mint and pomegranate seeds. Serve hot or cold.

132 TOMATO AND BASIL SALSA

1 medium tomato; coarsely
chopped
1 tablespoon finely diced red
onion
1 1/2 teaspoon minced seeded
Jalapeño

2 tablespoon balsamic vinegar
1/4 cup fresh basil chiffonade
1 1/2 teaspoon olive oil
salt to taste
freshly ground black pepper
to taste

Combine the tomato, onion, Jalapeño, vinegar, basil and olive oil.
Add salt and pepper to taste. Cover and Refrigerate for up to 1 day.
Bring to room temperature before serving. Serve any extra salsa in a
bowl in the center of the table.

133 JICAMA PEACH SALSA

1 cup peeled; diced jicama
1/4 cup chopped red onion
1/2 cup roasted; peeled,
chopped red bell pepper
2 medium peaches (or
nectarines); pitted, chopped

2 Jalapeño chilies; seeded,
chopped
3 tablespoon fresh lime juice
1/2 teaspoon Ancho chili
powder; or to taste

1 tablespoon chopped fresh   mint

In a medium glass bowl, combine the jicama, onion, red pepper, peaches, Jalapeños, lime juice, chili powder, and mint. Store in a covered container, in the refrigerator, no more than 1 day.

134 MINTED MANGO SALSA

1 large mango
1/2 red onion; finely chopped
3 teaspoon red aji paste
2 limes; juiced
1 1/2 teaspoon coarse salt

1 pinch freshly-ground black pepper
1/2 bunch mint leaves; chopped

Stand a mango upright and cut off four slices around the flat pit inside. Remove skin and cut mango into large pieces. In a blender combine mango with the onion, aji, lime juice, salt and pepper, and puree until smooth. Cover and Let stand for 1 hour. Stir in chopped mint.

135 SWEET POTATO APPLE SALSA

1 large red delicious apple; diced
1 small uncooked sweet potato; finely diced
2 green onions; white, tender green parts, thinly sliced

1 Jalapeño pepper; seeded and diced
2 tablespoon fresh lime or lemon juice
2 tablespoon honey

Combine all ingredients; blend well. cover; chill for one hour.

136 HUACHINANGO EN SALSA VERDE

1/2 cup onion coarsely chopped
2 tablespoons fresh cilantro chopped
2 fresh Jalapeños stems removed
1 13 ounce can tomatillo rinsed and drained
6 fresh hot green chilies

1/4 cup unsalted butter or more as needed
1/2 cup all-purpose flour
1/2 teaspoon salt
freshly ground black pepper to taste
6 to 8 ounce red snapper filets
hot cooked rice

To make the salsa verde: Place onion, cilantro, Jalapeños, and tomatillo in a blender or food processor and process until very smooth. set aside. Cut each green chile lengthwise, open out to make a flat sheet. set aside. preheat oven to 350. Melt butter in a skillet;

meanwhile combine flour, salt and pepper in a shallow, flat bottomed dish. Dip filets in flour mixture, then cook in butter, turning once, for about 5 minutes per side or until light golden brown. Wrap each fillet in a green chile. Arrange wrapped filets on an oven proof platter and top with salsa verde. Place in oven just until salsa and chilies are hot; then serve on warmed plates accompanied with rice.

137 CHILE GUAJILLO SALSA

1/2 pound dried guajillo chilies	1/2 pound Roma tomatoes
3 cups water	2 teaspoons toasted pumpkin seeds
5 large cloves garlic roasted	1/3 cup cider vinegar
1 teaspoon ground cumin	1 teaspoon ground Mexican oregano
1 teaspoon salt	

Remove stems and seeds from the guajillos. Place them in skillet or in a 250 oven and dry roast them for 3-4 minutes. Shake them once or twice and be careful not to scorch or they'll be bitter. Drop them into water that's been heated to just below the boiling point. use just enough water to cover chilies and press them down with a lid. Allow to sit for 20 minutes or until soft. Taste the water to see if it is bitter. If it is, discard it; if not, reserve for thinning salsa, if needed. Puree prepared chilies with remaining ingredients. Serve cold as a salsa or, to use as a sauce. Heat 2 tablespoons peanut oil or lard in a high-sided pan and refry sauce at a sizzle for 3 to 5 minutes, stirring continuously. Add a little water if necessary to get to proper consistency.

138 TOMATO AND CAPER SALSA

1 pound Roma tomatoes; finely diced	juice and zest of 1 lemon
2 handfuls rocket leaves	1 tablespoon drained capers; minced
1/2 cup olive oil	1 ounce Kalamata olives; stoned and chopped
1 shallot; chopped	
2 cloves garlic; minced	

Combine the diced tomatoes, rocket leaves, olive oil, shallots, garlic, lemon juice and zest, capers and olives in a mixing bowl and toss well. Season to taste with salt and pepper if desired. Set aside. (acidic ingredients will wilt the rocket leaves)

139 LEMON BALM SALSA

2 tablespoon sunflower seeds	8 sun-dried tomatoes; chopped
1 medium red onion; coarsely chopped	3 tablespoon lemon balm leaves; chopped

salt and black pepper
1 lemon; juice of

6 tablespoon olive oil; (6 to 8)

Toss the sunflower seeds in a hot frying pan without oil, dry roast them until slightly browned. Grind them coarsely. Mix with all the other ingredients for the salsa. Put it in the refrigerator and allow at least 30 minutes for the flavors to blend before serving.

140 SALSA BORRACHA HERRADURA

6 Serrano chilies en escabeche, rinsed, stems removed, chopped
2 tablespoon oil
1 large onion, chopped

3 cloves garlic, minced
1/2 cup lime juice
1/4 cup water
1/4 cup tequila
1/4 teaspoon ground cloves

Put it all in a blender and puree until smooth. Serving suggestions:... as a marinade for barbequed or grilled meats or poultry, or as a condiment with grilled meat, poultry or fish.

141 SALSA XCATIC

9 xcatic chilies finely chopped
1 medium white onions finely chopped
1/4 cup vegetable oil

1/2 teaspoon salt
2 tablespoon white vinegar
freshly ground black pepper
to taste

Sauté the chilies and onion in the oil for 20 minutes at low heat. Place in a blender with the remaining ingredients and puree until smooth.

142 CONGO PEPPER SALSA

5 Congo peppers, stemmed and seeded
1 cup water
1/2 teaspoon salt

1 onion minced
2 clove garlic minced
1/4 cup fresh cilantro minced

Puree the peppers with the water in a blender. Add the remaining ingredients and Let the mixture sit for at least an hour to blend the flavors. Serve with grilled meats, poultry, or fish.

143 BUTT KICKIN BEER SALSA

1/2 cup butter; 1 stick
1 onion; finely chopped
1 garlic clove; finely chopped
3 tablespoon vinegar
1 cup chili sauce

1 cup water
pepper
2 tablespoon brown sugar
2 tablespoon Worcestershire sauce

1/2 tablespoon mustard
1/2 lemon; juice
1 can beer

2 tablespoon Tabasco sauce
1 chopped Habañero pepper

In a large saucepan, sauté onion and garlic in butter. When the onions are transparent Add the remainder of ingredients. Bring to a boil. Simmer until your grill is ready, about 10 to 15 minutes or until you can not stand the wonderful smell of the sauce any longer.

144 AGENT ORANGE HABAÑERO PEPPER SALSA

12 Habañero peppers, stems removed
1/2 cup chopped onion
2 cloves garlic, minced

1 tablespoon vegetable oil
1/2 cup chopped carrots
1/2 cup distilled vinegar
1/4 cup lime juice

Sauté the onion and garlic in oil until soft. Add the carrots with a small amount of water. Bring to a boil, reduce heat and simmer until carrots are soft. Place the mixture and raw chilies into a blender and puree until smooth. Do not Cook the peppers, since cooking reduces flavor of the Habañeros. Combine the puree with vinegar and lime juice, then simmer for 5 minutes and seal in sterilized bottles.

145 RUM HABAÑERO SALSA

1/2 cup rum and 1 cup sherry
1 or 2 Habañeros or Serranos
5 allspice berries

2 or 3 cloves
20 or so mustard seeds

Let it sit for a couple of weeks for the flavor to develop. The rum version is tastes very Caribbean.

146 WINE HABAÑERO SALSA

20 Habañeros
1 large chipotle in adobo sauce
1 white onion, chopped
2 garlic cloves, chopped
1 teaspoon ground cumin

1 tablespoon lemon juice
1/2 apple, peeled
1 teaspoon salt
1/4 cup distilled white vinegar
1 tablespoon lemon juice
3/4 cup white wine

Stem and seed the Habañeros, leaving the inner membranes. Combine the Habañeros with all the other ingredients except the lemon juice and wine in a blender and process to a fine puree. Transfer to a non-reactive pan and cook over low-medium heat for ten minutes. Add lemon juice and wine, mix well and transfer to sterilized sauce bottles.

147 THREE T☺MAT☺ SALSA

3 large plum tomatoes, diced
3 large yellow tomatoes, diced
3 large green tomatoes, diced
half a small cucumber, diced
2 spring onions, finely chopped
1 garlic clove, finely chopped
1 large red, green and yellow chili deseeded and finely chopped
juice of 1 lime
3 tablespoon virgin olive oil
1 tablespoon caster sugar
1 teaspoon salt
deep fried flour tortilla quarters, tossed in smoked paprika and salt or corn chips

Place all the ingredients in a bowl and mix them together until combined. Set the salsa aside fro 30 minutes before serving. The salsa is best served in 1-2 hours after preparing but can be made up to a day in advance and refrigerated then brought to room temperature before serving. Serve the salsa with deep fried tortilla wedges or corn chips.

148 SALSA BORRACHA

6 pasilla chilies
1 cup beer or pulque (a fermented corn beverage)
juice of 1 orange
1 cup love garlic
1/4 medium onion, finely chopped
10 whole green olives
1/2 cup crumbled whole ite cheese (queso fresco)

Place a heavy duty skillet over a medium flame. Toast the pasilla chilies in the skillet until the skin blisters. Open the chilies and remove the stems, veins, and seeds. Soak the chilies in the beer for 30 minutes. Place the beer and chilies in a blender or food processor along with the peeled garlic clove and the orange juice. Puree until smooth. Stir in the chopped onion and add salt to taste. Before serving place the olives and the crumbled cheese into the salsa for garnish.

149 CHICKPEA SALSA

1/2 pound (about 1 1/4 cup) dried chickpeas, or 2 1/2 cup canned
2 1/4 teaspoon salt, plus more to taste
1/4 teaspoon cumin seeds or 1/2 teaspoon ground cumin
1 clove garlic, peeled
2 teaspoon extra-virgin olive oil
4 small dried chilies, stemmed and finely chopped, or 3/4 teaspoon red-pepper flakes
1/2 cup oil-cured olives, pitted and coarsely chopped
1 teaspoon fresh lemon juice
freshly ground pepper
1 small bunch arugula

Pick over dried chickpeas. rinse and soak overnight in cold water with 1 teaspoon salt. Drain and rinse. Place chickpeas in a medium saucepan and cover by several inches with fresh water. Bring to a boil and skim off any foam. Turn heat down to medium and simmer until tender, 35 to 45 minutes. Ten minutes before chickpeas are done, add 3/4 teaspoon salt. Remove from heat; let cool in cooking liquid for about 1 hour. If using cumin seeds, toast in a dry pan over medium-low heat until they release their aroma, about 2 minutes. Let cool and grind to a powder in a spice grinder. set aside. Chop together 1/2 teaspoon salt, the garlic, and 1/2 teaspoon olive oil to form a paste. Add chilies; chop to combine. Transfer to a small bowl and add remaining oil. Drain soaked chickpeas. If using canned chickpeas, rinse. Combine with 1 teaspoon chile mixture, or to taste. Add olives, cumin, lemon juice, and salt and pepper to taste. Refrigerate until ready to Serve. the salsa can be made 1 day ahead (return to room temperature before serving). Just before serving, coarsely chop arugula and toss with salsa. Serve as a condiment with lamb or chicken.

150 STRAWBERRY RED SALSA

1/2 medium red onion thinly sliced	1/4 cup fresh cilantro finely shredded
1 whole Jalapeño pepper minced	1/2 pint fresh strawberries hulled sliced
1/2 whole red bell pepper stemmed, seeded julienned	1/4 cup fresh orange juice
1/2 whole yellow bell pepper stemmed, seeded julienned	2 tablespoons fresh lime juice
1/2 whole green pepper stemmed, seeded julienned	2 tablespoons extra virgin olive oil
	salt and pepper to taste

Place all the ingredients in a large mixing bowl and toss to combine. Cover and refrigerate at least 2 hours or up to 4 hours. fifteen minutes before serving, remove the salsa from the refrigerator.

151 ZUCCHINI AND HOMINY SALSA

1/4 cup onion chopped, 1 small	20 ounce hominy drained, 1 can
2 tablespoon butter	2 tablespoon lime juice
2 tablespoon vegetable oil	1 tablespoon chile powder
3 each zucchini medium.,	1 teaspoon salt
2 cup tomatoes chopped, 2 medium	1 dash pepper

Cook and stir the onion in the butter and oil in a 10-inch skillet over medium heat until tender. Stir in the remaining ingredients and cook uncovered, stirring occasionally, until the zucchini is tender, about 10 to 15 minutes

152 BERRY GOOD AVOCADO SALSA

2 tablespoon safflower oil
1 shallot; minced
3 tablespoon raspberry vinegar
1 tablespoon poppy seeds
1 teaspoon sugar

1 large avocado; peeled and pitted and cut into 1/2-inch cubes
1 pint fresh raspberries; halved if large
1 Poblano pepper; roasted, skinned and seeded and, minced

Heat oil in small saucepan over medium-high heat. Add the shallots and sauté for 1 minute, stirring frequently. Lower the heat to medium and add the vinegar, poppy seeds, and sugar. Continue cooking for 2 minutes, stirring constantly. Remove from the heat and let cool. Combine the avocado, raspberries, and chile in a medium bowl. Add the vinegar mixture to the bowl and fold gently to coat. Serve immediately. This salsa will not keep.

153 SALSA CORTEZ

20 large tomatoes or 60 Roma tomatoes
2 large onions, chopped
6 or 7 Jalapeño peppers
3 green chili peppers
4 cloves garlic, chopped

1 tablespoon. oregano
1 tablespoon. cumin
1 tablespoon. chili powder
1 1/2 tablespoon. salt
1/2 tablespoon. pepper

Chop up tomatoes after they have been blanched and peeled. Add onions, peppers and seasonings; cook on stove for about 45 minutes or until your desired consistency. Put in pint jars and water bath for 30 minutes or pressure for 10 minutes at 5 pounds pressure.

154 EXTRA HOT SALSA

5 (1 pound.) cans peeled tomatoes
20 diced sorano peppers
10 diced Jalapeño peppers
15 diced yellow squash
1 diced bell pepper

2 chopped onions (large)
2 tablespoon. minced garlic
1 (10 ounce.) can tomato juice
2 tablespoon. vinegar
1/8 cup. vegetable oil

Put oil into a large pot over a high heat. Put in chopped onions and garlic. Then add bell peppers after 10 minutes. Add the rest of the peppers; cook 10 minutes, stirring often. Add tomato juice and can tomatoes; cook for 1 hour over medium heat. When it cools, add 2 tablespoons vinegar to work as a preservative.

155 ZUCCHINI HOT SALSA

10 cup. ground zucchini
3 1/2 cup. ground onion
3 1/2 cup. ground hot peppers
(about 25) or to taste
6 tablespoon. salt
1 cup. brown sugar
2 cup. vinegar
5 cup. ground tomatoes
1 tablespoon. garlic powder

1 tablespoon. crushed red
pepper
1 tablespoon. nutmeg
1 tablespoon. coarse black
pepper
1 tablespoon. turmeric
1 tablespoon. cumin
1 tablespoon. cornstarch
2 tablespoon. dry mustard

Mix together the first 4 ingredients and let it stand overnight in cool place. Rinse and drain well. Mix the remaining ingredients well. Add the zucchini, onions and pepper; heat to boil and simmer for 30 minutes. Pack in hot jars; seal and process for 20 minutes in hot water bath.

156 SALSA ANCHOVY

2 tablespoon. pure olive oil
2 garlic cloves, minced
1 celery rib, minced
4 1/2 cup. crushed tomatoes
8 Anchovies, chopped

8 stuffed green peppers,
minced
8 pitted black olives, sliced
1 teaspoon. capers
1 teaspoon. fresh basil
1/4 teaspoon. red pepper

Heat oil in skillet. sauté garlic, celery and pepper until soft. Add tomatoes and Anchovies. Simmer for 10 minutes. Stir in olives, capers, basil and red pepper. Simmer, uncovered for 20 minutes. Serve with favorite pasta.

157 SALSA DE CHICARO

1 cup. cooked green peas
2 tomatoes, peeled, seeded
and chopped
3 tablespoon. finely chopped
onion
2 tablespoon. vinegar
2 tablespoon. oil
1 tablespoon. chopped capers

2 tablespoon. finely chopped
green pepper
2 tablespoon. chopped green
olives
1/4 teaspoon. thyme
1/2 teaspoon. salt
freshly ground black pepper

Place the peas and tomatoes in a bowl and mash with the back of a fork. Add the onion, vinegar and oil and beat vigorously. Blend in all the remaining ingredients. Serve the sauce with fish or veal.

158 PINEAPPLE PAPAYA MANGO SALSA

1 medium pineapple	1 tablespoon lime juice
1 large papaya	cayenne pepper; or Jalapeño
2 mangos	pepper minced
1 small white or red onion	pepper to taste

Dice fruits and onion into small pieces. Toss together in a bowl with lime juice. To spice up salsa, add a dash of cayenne pepper or minced Jalapeño pepper to taste. This should be done a hour before dinner to give a chance for the flavors to meld. Great way to liven up grilled or broiled meats, and fish and chicken.

159 HOT AND SPICY PUMPKIN SALSA

4 cup pumpkin pulp (about one 8-inch pie pumpkin)	1/2 cup coarsely chopped dark raisins
1 1/2 cup dark brown sugar	3 hot yellow peppers, seeded and chopped
1 1/4 cup malt vinegar	2 tablespoon minced garlic
1/2 cup coarsely chopped onion	2 tablespoon minced ginger
	1 teaspoon salt

Wash pumpkin, cut into large pieces, scrape out and discard seeds. Place pumpkin pieces in large saucepan; cover with water. Bring to boil; boil gently 20 minutes or until tender. Drain. Remove rind from pulp; mash pulp to uniform consistency. Measure 4 cups pulp into large stainless steel or enamel saucepan. Add sugar, vinegar, onions, raisins, peppers, garlic, ginger and salt. Bring to a boil; boil gently 45 minutes or until thick. Fill boiling water canner with water. Place 5 clean mason jars in canner over high heat. Prepare 2-piece metal lids according to manufacturer's directions. Ladle chutney into hot jar to within 1/2-inch of top rim (head space). Remove air bubbles by sliding rubber spatula between glass and food; readjust headspace. Wipe jar to remove any stickiness. Center lid on jar, apply screw band just until fingertip tight. Place filled jars in canner. Cover, return water to a boil and process 10 minutes. Remove jars. Cool 24 hours. Check jar seals. Sealed lids curve downward. wipe jars, label and store in a cool, dark place.

160 SQUASH SALSA

1 small zucchini (peeled)	3 Serrano chilies
1 small yellow squash (peeled)	1/2 each small red onion
1 carrot (peeled)	1 tablespoon finely chopped marjoram
2 tomatillo	4 teaspoon extra virgin olive oil
1 medium tomato	
1 clove garlic	

1 tablespoon unseasoned rice vinegar

1 tablespoon sugar
1 each salt to taste

Finely dice all, mix and let sit for an hour before serving.

161 SUMMER BREAKFAST SALSA

1 ripe mango, peeled, seeded and diced
5 strawberries, sliced and quartered
3 kiwi fruits, peeled, sliced and quartered
1/3 cup fresh blueberries

2 1/2 teaspoon sugar or to taste
2 teaspoon champagne
1/4 teaspoon freshly grated ginger root
7 medium-size mint leaves plus fresh mint sprigs for garnish

Place mango in a large bowl; Add strawberries, kiwi, blueberries, sugar, champagne, ginger root and chopped mint. taste and adjust sugar and ginger to taste. Garnish with fresh mint sprig and serve.

162 BLACK EYED PEA SALSA

3 cups cooked black-eyed peas
2 cups frozen corn, thawed
1/2 cup chopped celery
1/2 cup red bell pepper chopped
1/2 cup red onion, chopped

1/2 cup fresh cilantro, chopped
2 each Jalapeño, de veined, de seeded, finely chopped
1/2 cup seasoned rice wine vinegar
1/4 cup water
1/4 tablespoon. sugar

Mix the vinegar with the water. dissolve the sugar in the vinegar mixture. Place the remaining ingredients and the vinegar dressing in a very tightly covered container and shake until thoroughly mixed and the vegetables are coated. Refrigerate and allow it to marinate for at least 8 hours. Serve on New Year's Day for good luck.

163 HABAÑERO SALSA

2 tablespoon olive oil
1 medium onion chopped
1 green bell pepper chopped
1 red bell pepper chopped
1/2 cup chicken broth
4 chilies Habañero minced
6 medium tomatoes skinned and diced
2 can tomatoes diced
2 tablespoon lime juice

2 tablespoon lemon juice
1 teaspoon dried coriander leaf
1 teaspoon oregano
1 tablespoon sugar or honey optional
salt and pepper to taste
1/4 cup fresh parsley chopped
2 Anaheim chili pepper chopped

Sauté the onions, bell peppers, and Anaheim in the oil for a few minutes then add the chicken broth and sauté until the broth is about gone. Add the Habañeros, the diced tomatoes, lime and lemon juices, coriander, oregano, sugar, salt and pepper. Simmer for 20 or 30 minutes and add the parsley and simmer a few more minutes.

164 GREEN BEAN WALNUT AND FETA SALSA

1 1/2 pounds fresh green beans cut in half
3/4 cup olive oil
1/2 cup packed mint leaves
1/4 cup white vinegar
3/4 teaspoon salt

1/4 teaspoon ground pepper
1/2 teaspoon minced garlic
1 cup chopped walnuts
1 cup diced red onion
1 cup crumbled feta cheese

Bring 4 quarts of water to boil. Add green beans; cook until tender-crisp about 4 minutes. Drain well and immerse in ice water. Drain and pat dry. Finely chop mint leaves. Combine mint, oil, vinegar, salt, pepper, garlic in processor and blend well. Refrigerate. Arrange beans in shallow glass serving bowl. Sprinkle with nuts and onions. Just before serving, pour dressing over and toss.

165 TOO HOT FOR SATAN SALSA

white vinegar
10 Jalapeño peppers
5 thai peppers
1/4 cup cilantro
1 garlic clove
1 onion
1 green peppers

1 cucumber
6 large tomatoes
assorted spices--chili powder,
cayenne pepper, cumin,
oregano, paprika
tobacco sauce
salt and pepper

Dice the peppers, leavings the seeds for good hot taste. throw them in a bowl. Then dice tomatoes up, and throw them in the bowl. Next, dice onion, green pepper, and throw in bowl, along with cilantro. Mince the garlic and throw that in the bowl. Next, dice the cucumber and throw that in the bowl. Take extra spices, and throw them into the bowl to your taste. Toss about 1-2 tablespoons of white vinegar into the bowl. Next, get a big spoon and stir the bowl, mixing all the ingredients up. Let sit until next day, and stir again to mix all the tastes in the bowl.

166 CARROT SALSA

1 carrot, grated
4 teaspoon chopped fresh coriander or parsley

1 teaspoon lemon juice
1/2 teaspoon vegetable oil

In bowl, stir together carrot, fresh coriander, lemon juice and oil; set aside.

167 CRANBERRY TOMATO SALSA

2 cups cranberries
2 plum tomatoes, seeded, chopped
1/4 cup minced cilantro
2 green onions, minced

2 tablespoons fresh lime juice
1 tablespoon sugar
2 teaspoons minced seeded Jalapeño chile
1 garlic clove, minced

Cook berries in pot of boiling water until skins just begin to burst, about 1 1/2 minutes. Drain well. Transfer to bowl. Add tomatoes, cilantro, onions, lime juice, sugar, chile and garlic season with salt, pepper and more sugar, if desired. (can be made 6 hours ahead. Cover; chill. Serve at room temperature.)

168 MELLOW YELLOW SALSA

8 cups chopped yellow tomatoes
4 cups chopped yellow bell peppers
4 cups chopped yellow onions
4 minced, seeded hot yellow banana peppers

1/2 teaspoon garlic powder or 4 cloves of minced fresh garlic
1/4 cup vinegar
juice of 1/2 fresh lime
1 tablespoon cumin
2 tablespoon pickling salt
2 teaspoon chopped cilantro
1 teaspoon white pepper

In a food processor, puree one cup of the tomatoes along with the hot banana peppers, garlic, vinegar and the spices. Put this mixture in a pot with the remaining chopped ingredients. Under medium heat, bring to a low boil, stirring frequently to avoid scorching the vegetables, then cook until onions are translucent. Leave the pot covered to avoid the steam from escaping for juicier salsa.

169 BLUEBERRY SALSA

1 bag frozen blueberries
1/2 purple onion finely diced
2 cloves crushed garlic

1 2 Serrano peppers finely diced (Add to taste)
1 jigger tequila
1/2 jigger lime juice

Add all ingredients in the blender or food processor. Frappe until smooth.

170 GINGER APRICOT AND HIBISCUS SALSA

1/2 cup white wine
1/4 cup sugar

1/2 cup hibiscus flowers dried

1/2 cup ginger peeled and diced juice of 1 lemon
2 tablespoons walnut oil
2 shallots diced

2 cups apricots diced
2 tablespoons basil chopped
2 tablespoons mint chopped
2 teaspoons sea salt

Combine wine, sugar, hibiscus, ginger and lemon in a sauce pan and bring to a boil. Set aside and let ingredients steep for at least 15 minutes. Strain through a fine sieve without pressing, then and walnut oil, apricots, shallots, basil, mint and season with salt. Set aside.

171 PERSIMMON CILANTRO SALSA

1/4 cup chopped fresh cilantro
1 1/2 tablespoons minced red onion
1 tablespoon fresh lime juice

1 teaspoon minced Jalapeño pepper
2 ripe persimmons (10 ounces) peeled and coarsely chopped

Combine all ingredients in a bowl, and stir well. cover and chill.

172 MANGO TEQUILA SALSA

2 cup mango; diced and peeled
2/3 cup red bell pepper; finely chopped
3 tablespoon tequila
2 tablespoon orange juice

1 tablespoon Jalapeño pepper; seeded and minced
2 teaspoon fresh mint; chopped
1/4 teaspoon salt

Combine all salsa ingredients in a small bowl; stir well. Cover and chill.

173 SALSA PICANTE DE CHILE CHIPOTLE

4 chipotle chilies
3 pasilla negro chilies
4 cascabel chilies
1/4 teaspoon fresh ground black pepper
3/4 cup water
1/2 cup cider vinegar
1 clove garlic
4 each chipotle chilies, stemmed and quartered including seeds

3 pasilla negro chilies, stemmed and quartered including seeds
4 each cascabel chilies, stemmed and broken, including seeds
1/4 teaspoon fresh ground black pepper
3/4 cup water
1/2 cup cider vinegar or Japanese rice vinegar
1 clove garlic, smashed and quartered

Place the chilies and their seeds. In a small blender jar, add the garlic and the black pepper. Mix the vinegar and the water together and heat until the mixture is just ready to boil, and add it to the peppers. Tightly close the jar and let the ingredients steep for at least 1/2 an hour. Then puree until smooth. This makes a tangy, tasty and thick salsa. The rice vinegar makes a somewhat mellower salsa than the cider vinegar.

174 UNCOOKED TOMATO SALSA WITH OLIVES AND MOZZARELLA

3 tomatoes; medium
2 garlic cloves; large, mince
3 tablespoon capers; drained
1 1/2 teaspoon oregano; dried
1/3 cup oil; olive

18 olives; black pitted and sliced
6 ounce mozzarella cheese; diced

Combine sauce ingredients in non-corrosive bowl, set aside for 30 minute or more, up to 2 hours. Cook pasta and drain. return empty pot to turned off burner. Pour in drained pasta and toss. Cover with lid for 1 minute to let cheese soften. uncover and serve.

175 WATERMELON PICO DE GALLO SALSA

1 1/2 cup seedless watermelon cut in 1/4 inch dice
1/4 cup honeydew melon cut in 1/4 inch dice
1/4 cup cantaloupe cut in 1/4 inch dice
1/2 cup jicama diced
1/4 cup red onion cut in 1/4 inch dice

1 Jalapeño chile pepper chopped
2 tablespoon lime juice fresh
1/2 cup fresh cilantro leaves chopped
maple syrup to taste
1/2 teaspoon salt or to taste

Combine all ingredients in a medium bowl and mix lightly so as not to break up the watermelon. Serve immediately with grilled barbeque chicken breasts or another dish.

176 YOGURT SALSA

1 pound plum tomatoes
1 medium onion
1 Jalapeño pepper
1/4 cup plain low fat yogurt

1/2 cup fresh cilantro; chopped
1 pinch salt
1/4 teaspoon pepper

Core and dice tomatoes. Peel and chop onion. Seed and chop pepper. Combine tomatoes, onion, pepper, yogurt, cilantro, salt and pepper in the work bowl of a food processor or blender. Process by pulsing until coarsely chopped, but not pureed.

177 MONTEREY JACK SALSA

4 ounce can green chilies
1/4 pound shredded Monterey
jack
4 green onions, chopped
cheese

1 tomato, chopped
1/2 cup Italian salad dressing
1/4 cup fresh, chopped,
cilantro

Blend chilies, onions, tomato, cilantro, cheese and salad dressing. Let set for 30 minutes to allow flavors to blend.

178 FRESH GRAPE SALSA WITH GINGER

3 cup seedless red or green
grapes; roughly chopped or
quartered
1/3 cup finely chopped red
onion
2 tablespoon chopped cilantro
2 tablespoon lime juice

1 1/2 teaspoon sugar
1 teaspoon balsamic vinegar;
up to 2
1 clove fresh garlic; finely
chopped
1 teaspoon grated fresh ginger
1/4 teaspoon salt

Combine all ingredients in a bowl and chill at least two hours before serving. Good with chicken, fish, beef or pork. Fruit salsas are best when freshly made, but they will keep up to 48 hours in the refrigerator.

179 MIXIOTE DE POLLO SALSA

6 Ancho chilies
8 guajillo chilies
4 pasilla chilies
2 teaspoon coarse salt; plus
more
1/8 teaspoon dried marjoram
1/8 teaspoon cumin seeds
1/2 teaspoon dried oregano
1 dried bay leaf

1/8 teaspoon dried thyme
8 whole cloves
4 cloves garlic
2 teaspoon coarse salt
1 tablespoon white vinegar
3 chicken drumsticks
3 chicken thighs
3 fresh avocado leaves
fresh tortillas; for serving

Toast chilies in a dry, hot skillet over medium-high heat until pliable, about 3 to 5 minutes; turn often to prevent burning. Remove seeds and veins from chilies and discard. Soak each type of chile separately in hot, salted water to cover for about 20 minutes. Drain, and reserve liquid. Grind marjoram, cumin seeds, oregano, bay leaf, thyme, and cloves in a spice grinder. In batches, combine drained chilies, ground herbs, garlic, salt, vinegar, and 1/2 cup soaking liquid in blender. Transfer to a large bowl. Add chicken, and marinate for at least 1 hour, preferably overnight. Cut three 16- by 16-inch parchment-paper squares. Place a drumstick, thigh, and an avocado leaf in the center of each square. Bring the four corners together, and tie with string. Place in a steamer, and steam over simmering water for 1 hour. To serve, remove string, and open parchment paper, folding under slightly. Serve with fresh, warm tortillas.

180 MELON PINEAPPLE SALSA

1 1/2 cup diced cantaloupe; honeydew or other melon
1/2 cup diced fresh pineapple
1 teaspoon seeded and minced Serrano chile
1/4 cup finely diced red onion
2 tablespoon olive oil
1/2 teaspoon finely minced garlic
1 tablespoon raspberry vinegar
1 tablespoon fresh lemon or lime juice
1/2 teaspoon honey
kosher salt; to taste
freshly ground black pepper to taste
2 tablespoon minced fresh cilantro

Gently combine the melon, pineapple, Serrano and onion in a bowl. In a separate bowl, whisk together the olive oil, garlic, vinegar, lemon juice and honey. Season to taste with salt and pepper. Just before serving, combine the oil mixture with the fruit and gently toss with the cilantro.

181 SPICY CITRUS SALSA

2 oranges; peeled and sectioned
2 lemons; peeled and sectioned
2 limes; peeled and sectioned
1 grapefruit; peeled and sectioned
1 red onion; julienned
1 fresh Jalapeño; diced
2 cloves garlic; chopped
2 teaspoon chopped gingerroot
2 tablespoon seasoned rice vinegar
3 tablespoon vegetable oil
1/2 teaspoon soy sauce; or to taste

In medium sized bowl, combine all ingredients; mix well. Place in covered container; chill until ready to serve.

182 WARM PLUM SALSA

4 large plums pitted, diced 1/4 inch
1 large garlic clove minced
2 tablespoon sugar
2 tablespoon balsamic vinegar
1/2 teaspoon salt
1/2 teaspoon sesame seeds for garnish

In a medium sauce pan, combine all ingredients except sesame seeds; cook over high heat for 3 minutes. Reduce heat to medium high and cook, stirring occasionally, until liquid thickens and the plums have softened and broken down to the consistency of a chunky. Preserve, about 15 minutes. Remove from heat, transfer plum sauce to a serving dish and sprinkle with sesame seeds. Serve warm.

183 MARGARITA JALAPEÑO SALSA

1/2 cup cubed tomato, 1/2 inch cubes
1/2 cup chopped red or white onion

4 each or more copped Jalapeños
1 each clove garlic, minced
1/2 teaspoon salt
1/4 cup gold or white tequila

A splash of tequila makes all the difference in this robust salsa; it has a way of mellowing the searing nature of terrifically hot foods. I like this sauce on seafood, chicken, and any king of chops pork, veal or lamb. Combine all ingredients and let stand for at least 30 minutes at room temperature. taste and adjust seasonings.

184 RED AND GREEN FIRE SALSA

1 small tomato; seeded, chopped
3/4 cucumber; peeled, seeded chopped
1/2 cup diced green bell pepper

1/2 cup sour cream
1/4 cup chopped fresh cilantro
1 1/2 tablespoon minced red Jalapeño
1 1/2 tablespoon minced green Jalapeño

Combine all ingredients in medium bowl. Season to taste with salt.

185 STRAWBERRY MANGO SALSA

1 cup diced strawberries
1/2 cup diced mango
1/4 cup diced yellow bell pepper
2 tablespoon fresh lime juice
1 tablespoon minced chives

1 tablespoon chopped cilantro
1 tablespoon olive oil
1 tablespoon red-wine vinegar
1 teaspoon minced fresh chile
salt and freshly ground black pepper

Combine all of the ingredients in a bowl and refrigerate for 1 hour. Serve cold or at room temperature.

186 NOPALITO SALSA

1 1/3 cup canned or bottled nopalitos rinsed, drained, diced or 1 1/3 cups diced cooked green beans
3/4 cup diced peeled jicama
2 small tomatoes; diced
1/3 cup diced onion

1/4 cup chopped fresh cilantro
3 tablespoon red wine vinegar
1 tablespoon olive oil
1 Serrano chili or small Jalapeño chili; minced
1 garlic clove; minced

Combine all ingredients in medium bowl. Season to taste with salt and pepper. Cover and refrigerate until well chilled, about 2 hours (Can be prepared 6 hours ahead. Keep refrigerated)

187 SESAME EGGPLANT SALSA

2 eggplants; (1 to 1 1/4 pound)
1 tablespoon vegetable oil or peanut oil
3/4 cup plus 1 tablespoon minced green onions; (packed)
2 1/2 tablespoon minced peeled fresh ginger
4 garlic cloves; minced
1 teaspoon chili-garlic sauce
3 tablespoon golden brown sugar; (packed)
2 tablespoon soy sauce
1 tablespoon rice vinegar
2 teaspoon fresh lemon juice
2 large plum tomatoes; seeded chopped
3/4 cup plus 1 tablespoon finely chopped fresh; (packed) cilantro
1 1/2 teaspoon oriental sesame oil
parmesan pita crisps

Preheat oven to 425. Pierce eggplants all over with fork. Place on baking sheet. Roast in oven until eggplants are very soft and deflated, turning once, about 1 hour. cool slightly. Cut eggplants in half; scrape flesh into strainer set over large bowl (do not allow bottom of strainer to touch bowl). Let eggplant drain 30 minutes. Transfer eggplant to processor. using on/off turns, process until almost smooth. Heat vegetable oil in heavy large skillet over medium-high heat. Add 3/4 cup green onions, ginger, garlic and chili-garlic sauce; sauté just until onions soften, about 45 seconds. Stir in brown sugar, soy sauce, vinegar and lemon juice. bring to simmer, stirring constantly. Mix in eggplant puree and cook until heated through, about 2 minutes. Remove from heat. Stir in tomatoes, 3/4 cup cilantro and sesame oil. cool to room temperature. Season with salt and pepper. Transfer to medium bowl. (can be prepared 1 day ahead. Cover and refrigerate. Bring to room temperature before serving.) Garnish eggplant salsa with 1 tablespoon each green onions and cilantro. Serve with parmesan pita crisps.

188 WINTER FRUIT SALSA

12 dried apricot halves; diced (1/3 cup)
4 dried calimyrna figs; stemmed and diced
1/3 cup water
2 tablespoon brandy; (optional)
1 tablespoon sugar
1/2 teaspoon ground coriander
1 pinch hot red pepper flakes
1 granny smith apple
1 tablespoon white vinegar
1/4 cup orange juice
1 rib celery; chopped
1/4 cup thinly sliced scallion
2 tablespoon chopped cilantro

1/4 teaspoon salt

In small saucepan, Combine apricots, figs, water, brandy, sugar, coriander, and pepper flakes. Bring to a boil; reduce heat to low, cover and simmer for 5 minutes, stirring occasionally. Cool to room temperature. At least 30 minutes before serving, core and dice apple and toss with vinegar and orange juice. Add to cooked fruits with celery, scallion, cilantro, and salt. Mix well. Serve at room temperature with ham.

189 NACHO MAMA SALSA

1 can whole tomatoes	fresh cilantro
1 yellow onion; (chopped)	1 can green chili peppers
1 clove minced garlic	1 dash salt

Put all ingredients in the food processor and mix on high for a few moments. Pour into dish and chill. Serve with chips.

190 AVOCADO ORANGE SALSA

3/4 cup orange segments	1/4 cup finely diced red onion
3/4 cup avocado; peeled, seeded, and cut into 1/2 inch cubes	1/4 cup chopped cilantro
	1 pinch dried red pepper flakes
juice of two limes	salt; to taste

Combine all ingredients and toss gently.

191 CACTUS SALSA

1 jar nopalitos (cactus) (12 ounce)	1 jalapeño
	2 green onions
1 small jicama	1/3 bunch cilantro
2 tomatoes	1/2 teaspoon salt

Rinse the nopalitos well, and cut into small pieces, about the size of a corn kernel. Place the cactus in a bowl. Peel the jicama and dice. Add the jicama to the cactus. Cut the tomatoes in half and remove the seeds. Chop the tomatoes and add to the cactus and jicama mix. Cut the meat off the jalapeño, discard the skin, mince, and add to cactus mix. Mince the green onions and cilantro, and add to mix. Add salt and blend well. Chill and serve.

192 LEMON CUCUMBER SALSA

1 cup cucumber; peeled and diced	2 tablespoon minced jalapeño peppers
1/4 cup red onion	1/4 cup red wine vinegar
3/4 cup diced Roma tomatoes	1 tablespoon chopped fresh mint

juice of half a lime   salt and pepper; to taste

Combine all ingredients in a bowl.

193 CORN AND SIX PEPPER SALSA

1 1/2 quart kernel sweet corn
1 cup diced green bell peppers
1 cup diced red bell peppers
1 cup diced yellow bell
peppers
6 diced fresh Jalapeño
peppers

1/2 cup diced banana peppers
6 diced green chili peppers
1/2 cup diced red onion
2 cup diced ripe tomatoes
1/2 cup chopped green onions
1 ounce cup chopped cilantro
3 cup spicy salsa

Combine all ingredients in a large mixing bowl. toss until completely
mixed. Refrigerate until served. recommend making one day ahead to
allow for maximum flavor.

194 NOPALITO CACTUS TEQUILA SALSA

1 nopalito cactus; diced small,
thorns
1/2 cup mixed peppers; sweet
and hot, diced
1/2 cup mixed citrus supremes
chopped (orange/grapefruit)
1/2 cup diced tomatoes
1 tablespoon chives; sliced

3 tablespoon cilantro;
chopped
2 tablespoon onion; diced
juice of 2 limes
2 tablespoon olive oil
(substitute 1 teaspoon oil; and
1 teaspoon broth or juice)
salt and pepper
1/2 cup tequila

Mix all together and chill before serving.

195 ROASTED PEPPER SALSA

3 red bell peppers; roasted
peeled and diced
3 cloves garlic; chopped
1/4 cup tomato puree
1 small red onion; diced
1/4 cup chopped fresh basil
2 tablespoon red wine vinegar

3 tablespoon olive oil
2 Anaheim chilies; roasted
peeled and diced
1/2 teaspoon dried coriander
1/2 teaspoon chili powder
salt and pepper to taste

In a large bowl, toss together the bell peppers, garlic, tomato puree,
red onion, and basil. Add vinegar, olive oil, and chilies, and mix well.
Season with coriander, chile powder, salt and pepper. Let stand for
about 30 minutes before serving.

196 UNCOOKED TOMATILLO TABLE SALSA

10 tomatillo papery husks removed; washed of their sticky surfaces, and cored
1 medium white onion; coarsely chopped

3 Jalapeño or Serrano chilies stemmed and coarsely chopped
8 cilantro sprigs chopped
1/2 teaspoon kosher salt
8 grinds of black pepper

Bring salted water to a boil. Drop in the tomatillo and boil for 1 minute. Do not overcook. Drain and chop. Place tomatillo, onion, chilies, cilantro, salt, and pepper in a blender. Blend to a coarse puree. Taste for seasoning and serve at room temperature.

197 FRESH SALSA MEXICANA FROM JUAREZ

1 Poblano chili; seeded and veined, finely chopped
1 red Jalapeño pepper; seeded and veined, finely chopped
2 yellow chilies; seeded and veined, finely chopped
2 Serrano peppers; finely chopped

3 tablespoon white onions; finely chopped
1 medium ripe tomato; finely chopped
1/2 cup water
3 tablespoon fresh lime juice
1/2 teaspoon dried oregano
salt; to taste

Mix all the ingredients together in a bowl; season with salt to taste. Set aside to macerate for about 1 hour.

198 GARLIC LOVERS SALSA CRUDA

1 large onion; finely minced
6-7 cloves garlic minced
2 teaspoon olive oil
6 tomatillo, finely chopped
1 tablespoon ground cumin
1/2 tablespoon ground coriander

28 ounce can whole tomatoes; drained and chopped
8 ounce can tomato sauce
2 tablespoon red wine vinegar
2 tablespoon minced fresh cilantro

Place onion and garlic in a large microwave-safe bowl and toss with oil. Microwave on high for 2 minutes. Add tomatillo, cumin, and coriander and microwave on high for 1 minute. Stir in tomatoes, tomato sauce, vinegar, and cilantro.

199 SALSA SURPRISE

2 1/2 cup vegetable broth or water
2 cup instant brown rice
1/4 cup minced onion
1 tablespoon butter

1/2 teaspoon salt
1/4 teaspoon ground coriander
4 cup or 15 ounce can kidney; pinto or pink beans, drained
1/2 cup canned or frozen corn

1 cup salsa   3/4 cup shredded Monterey
                               Jack cheese

Bring the stock to a boil in a large saucepan over medium-high heat.
Stir in rice, onion, butter, salt and coriander and return to boil.
Reduce heat, cover and simmer 10 minutes or until the water is
absorbed. Stir in the beans, corn and salsa into the rice. Cover and
steam an additional 2 to 3 minutes, or until heated through. Turn rice
mixture into a 13 x 9 inch shallow casserole dish, spreading evenly
without packing. Sprinkle with cheese and place under broiler until
the cheese is melted.

200 AUTUMN BLACK BEAN SALSA

1 large sweet potato baked   1/4 cup fresh parsley;
and peeled   chopped
2 cup cooked or canned black   1/4 cup fresh sage; chopped
beans; drained   2 teaspoon ground coriander
1 red onion; peeled and diced   1/8 teaspoon ground cayenne
1 clove garlic; minced   pepper
1 yellow or orange bell   kosher salt to taste
pepper; seeded and diced   grated sharp cheddar cheese
1 Jalapeño; seeded and diced   for garnish
1 red apple; cored and diced   toasted pumpkin seeds; for
1/4 cup apple cider vinegar   garnish
1 lime; juice of

Divide the sweet potato, placing half in a mixing bowl, and mash
until smooth. Dice the remaining half and add to the bowl. Add the
remaining ingredients and combine well. allow the salsa to rest for a
minimum of 6 hours. Top with a sprinkling of cheese and pumpkin
seeds just before serving.

Appetizer Primer:

Heat and eat gourmet treats for holiday and seasonal entertaining,
include hors d'oeuvres (snacks you eat with a fork), canapés
(anything spread on an edible base), salsas (sauces or dips), and
festive finger foods. They are great for cocktail and buffet parties.
Hors d'oeuvres mean "outside of the meal," so they are not served
with the entrée. Frequently they are the only item served at parties.
Canapés are spread on edible bases, such as assorted crackers, cream
cheese pastry, party rye, puff pastry, savory toast, or pita wedgies.
Toppings are limited only to your imagination, but favorites include
anchovies, aspic, bacon bits, capers, caviar, cheese, crab meat, egg,
lobster bits, mushrooms, nuts, olives, onions, oysters, paprika,
parsley, peppers, pimientos, radishes, shrimp, and tomatoes. Salsas

are popular year-round, and festive finger foods can help create a lively party atmosphere.

Bonus Recipes

201 CHEROKEE "WAR-HOOP" SOUP

1 lb. ground beef	2 c. cubed potatoes
1/2 c. bread crumbs	1 c. chopped celery
1 egg	1 c. chopped onion
1/2 tsp. salt	1/2 c. carrot, sliced
1 tsp. Tabasco sauce	3 beef bouillon cubes
3 c. water	1 tsp. Tabasco sauce
2 c. whole kernel corn	1 (16 oz.) jar Cheez Whiz

Make tiny nickel size meatballs with ground beef, bread crumbs, egg, salt and Tabasco sauce, set aside. In large pot, add water, corn, potato, celery, onion, carrot, bouillon cubes and Tabasco sauce. Boil for 5 minutes. Add meatballs, stir gently. Simmer, covered, for 2 hours. Gently stir in Cheez Whiz just before serving. Serve with saltine or oyster crackers.

202 CHEROKEE CHICKEN

2 lb. chicken pieces	1 can whole cranberry sauce
1/2 c. chopped onions	2 to 3 tsp. dry vermouth
1/2 c. sliced mushrooms	

Saute chicken pieces in skillet about 5 minutes on each side. Remove. Add onions and mushrooms. Saute until tender. Add cranberry sauce and vermouth. Mix well. When cranberry sauce has become liquid, add chicken pieces. Cover and simmer about 45 minutes.

203 CHEROKEE CASSEROLE

1 lb. beef, ground	1/2 bay leaf
1 Tbsp. olive oil	1 (1 lb.) can tomatoes
3/4 c. onions	1 can mushroom soup
1 1/2 tsp. salt	1 c. rice
dash of pepper	6 olives
1/8 tsp. garlic powder	2 to 3 slices cheese, cut in 1/2
1/8 tsp. oregano	strips
1/8 tsp. thyme	

Brown meat in oil; add onions. Mix ingredients, except olives and cheese. Bring to a boil. Reduce heat and simmer for 5 minutes; stir occasionally. Spoon into baking dish and top with cheese and olives.

204 CHEROKEE POTATOES

6 large potatoes, peeled and sliced thin
2 tsp. salt
pepper to taste
2 large onions, peeled and sliced thin
1 medium-size can tomatoes or 4 to 5 large tomatoes, cut small
1/2 c. shortening
1 Tbsp. vinegar
1 tsp. chili powder

A large iron skillet is best for this. Fry potatoes until browned (half down). Drain off excess fat. Add tomatoes, onions, salt and pepper to potatoes. Cover and simmer 10 minutes. Add vinegar and chili powder; stir easily. Heat until bubbly, about 5 minutes.

205 CHEROKEE WAMPUS BREAD

1 c. cornmeal
1/2 c. flour
1 tsp. salt
1 1/2 tsp. baking powder
1 tsp. sugar
1/2 c. evaporated milk
1/2 c. grated onion
1/2 c. grated raw potato

Mix until smooth. Drop by teaspoonfuls in pan of hot shortening (about 1 1/2-inches deep). Fry until golden brown. Serve warm. This is quick to make and goes especially well with fish.

206 CHEROKEE YAM CAKES

2 c. sifted flour
1 1/2 tsp. sugar
1 1/2 tsp. salt
2 1/2 tsp. soda
1/2 c. sweet milk
1 c. mashed sweet potatoes

Sift flour, baking powder, sugar and salt into a bowl. Pour oil and milk into a measuring cup but do not stir. Add to yams. Blend well. Add to flour mixture and mix lightly with a fork until mixture holds together. Turn dough out onto floured board and knead gently until smooth, about 12 strokes. Roll dough about 1/4-inch thick and cut into rounds with biscuit cutter. Place on a baking dish. Bake at 425 degrees for 10 to 20 minutes.

207 CRAB PARMESAN HORS D'OEUVRE

3/4 c. mayonnaise
1 large onion, finely chopped
1 1/2 c. Parmesan cheese, grated
1 can Alaska king crab

Mix all together; spread on party rye bread. Broil until golden brown. Serve hot. Makes 40 hors d'oeuvres.

208 CHILI CHEESE HORS D'OEUVRES

1/2 c. butter or margarine
10 eggs
1/2 c. flour
1/4 tsp. salt
1 tsp. baking powder
1 (8 oz.) can chopped green chilies
1 pt. cottage cheese

1 lb. Jack or Cheddar cheese   grated

Melt butter in pan, set aside. Beat eggs until light. Add flour, baking powder, salt and melted butter. Mix well. Add chilies, cottage cheese and Jack cheese. Stir together and pour into greased 13 x 9-inch pan. Bake in 400 degrees oven for 15 minutes, then 350 degrees for 35 minutes more. Cut very small and serve hot as hors d'oeuvres.

209 ONION HORS D'OEUVRES

8 oz. sharp cheddar cheese
12 oz. pkg. frozen onions, chopped
3 c. Bisquick

2 c. milk
2 eggs
1/4 lb. butter
poppy seed

Saute onions in 4 tablespoons butter. Combine Bisquick, milk and eggs. Add onions and 1/2 of the grated cheese. Pour into greased 9 x 13-inch pan. Sprinkle rest of grated cheese on top. Drizzle 4 tablespoons butter over mixture and sprinkle poppy seed on top. Bake in 400 degrees oven for 20 minutes. Cut into 1 1/2-inch squares as hors d'oeuvres. (If frozen, heat covered with foil; if Pyrex dish, bake at 375 degrees.)

210 TOSTITOS (HORS D'OEUVRES)

1 can refried beans (15 oz.)
1 jar taco sauce (8 oz)
1 lb. ground beef, browned and drained

1 (8 oz.) Cheddar cheese, shredded plus more for garnish
sour cream

Spread beans on the bottom of 10-inch pie plate (as if to form a crust); add meat, cheese; spread taco sauce over top. Bake 20 minutes at 350 degrees. Top with small amount of shredded cheddar as a garnish and also garnish with dollops of sour cream to your liking. Dip Tostitos into middle and serve as hors d'oeuvres. If you like onion flavor, you can fry with ground beef or just dice some fine (raw) and put in with beef mixture.

211 MEXICAN HORS D'OEUVRES

2 cans Mexican bean dip
1/2 c. mayonnaise
1 c. sour cream
1 pkg. taco seasoning mix
2 avocados
juice of 1/2 lemon
1/4 c. mayonnaise

2 tomatoes, chopped and drained
2 cans sliced black olives
1 bunch scallions, chopped
1 c. finely shredded Cheddar cheese
tortilla chips

On a serving platter spread a layer of bean dip. Mix together 1/2 cup mayonnaise, sour cream and taco seasoning mix. Spread over bean layer but keep within 1/2 inch all around sides of bean dip (pyramid effect). Mash 2 avocados with lemon juice and 1/4 cup mayonnaise. Add this layer on top but within 1/2 inch of sour cream layer. Mix together tomatoes, olives and scallions; put on top of last layer. Top with cheese. Serve with tortilla chips to dip through all layers of Mexican dip.

212 HERBED CHEESE

8 oz. small curd cottage cheese
4 oz. cream cheese, softened
1 c. fresh parsley
1 clove garlic

3 to 4 fresh chives (or 1 Tbsp. frozen chopped chives)
1/2 tsp. thyme
1/4 tsp. basil

Combine all ingredients in a blender or a food processor. Blend until creamy and smooth. Line a small bowl with either cheese cloth or plastic wrap (to help in the un-molding process) and spoon mixture into it. Pack it in firmly and cover with plastic wrap. Chill overnight for best results. To Serve: Un-mold onto serving dish about 1 hour before hors d'oeuvres are to be served. Arrange with pieces of endive, celery, carrots, stoned wheat, rye or pumpernickel crackers. Also yummy when stuffed into cherry tomatoes!

213 MEAT BALL HORS D'OEUVRES

2 lb. hamburger
1/3 c. parsley flakes
2 Tbsp. soy sauce
1/2 tsp. garlic juice
2 Tbsp. minced onion

1 c. corn flake crumbs
2 eggs, beaten
1/4 tsp. pepper
1/3 c. catsup

Sauce:
1 can cranberry sauce
2 Tbsp. brown sugar

1 (12 oz.) jar chili sauce
1 Tbsp. lemon juice

Mix meat ball ingredients in small balls, about 1-inch size. May be frozen at this point. Place meat balls in baking pan. Make sauce and pour over. Bake at 350 degrees about 30 minutes.

214 SAUSAGE CANAPÉS

1 lb. ground sausage
1 medium onion

1 egg
2 c. Cheddar cheese

Mix all ingredients until mixture resembles meat loaf. Spread on small rye rounds. Bake at 350 degrees for 10 to 12 minutes until sausage is done.

215 CANAPÉ CUT-OUTS

thin sliced bread   sherry

Let bread dry. Remove crusts and cut into small fingers, triangles, diamond shapes or cut with canapé cutter. Dip shapes quickly into sherry. Place on greased baking sheet. Bake in moderate oven at 375 degrees until crisp and brown. Remove to cooling rack. Store in airtight container if not used right away. Use as base for canapé spreads.

216 HOT BELL PEPPER CANAPÉ

extra thin sliced bread   1/4 lb. butter, room
1/2 lb. Blue cheese, room   temperature
temperature   1 medium bell pepper

Remove crust from bread and cut into 3 strips. Mix cheese and butter. Chop pepper very fine and add to cheese and butter mixture. Spread on bread strips. Put strips on cookie sheet and bake at 350 degrees until bread does not blend when picked up.

217 PECAN CANAPÉ

Use very large pecans. Make filling of cream cheese, Roquefort cheese and mayonnaise. Squeeze in a few drops of lemon juice. Mix well. Put between pecan halves. Refrigerate to make firm.

218 HOT MUSHROOM CANAPÉ

1 (8 oz.) pkg. cream cheese   pinch baking soda
1 egg yolk   2 cans button mushrooms
1/4 tsp. minced onion   bread

Cut bread any shape. Toast on one side. Put melted butter on other side. Cream the cream cheese, egg yolk, onion and baking soda. Put one mushroom on small piece of bread and top with mixture. Broil for 2 to 5 minutes. Serve hot.

219 CHEDDAR-HAM CANAPÉS

1 lb. sharp Cheddar cheese,   1 small bottle pimento-stuffed
grated   olives, chopped
1 c. cooked ham   1 large onion, chopped
1 (8 oz.) can tomato sauce   3 drops Tabasco sauce
1 medium green pepper,
chopped

Thoroughly mix together all ingredients and refrigerate. Make canapé bases from sliced bread, using small round cutter. To prevent bases from absorbing, put on a cookie sheet and place under the broiler until light brown. Spread mixture generously on broiled side of canapé. Place on cookie sheet and again under the broiler just long enough for cheese to melt, about 2 minutes.

Anchovy Butter:
6 Tbsp. butter   2 Tbsp. anchovy paste
Cream together butter with anchovy paste or with pounded
fillet of anchovy. Strain through a fine sieve and chill.

Chive Butter:
2 Tbsp. salted butter   chervil, tarragon, chives,
1/2 tsp. finely chopped pard   shallots
Mix together chervil, tarragon, chives and shallots and cream them
with 2 tablespoons of salted butter.

Deviled Butter:
3 Tbsp. butter   1/4 tsp. Tabasco sauce
1 tsp. dry mustard   1 tsp. each grated onion and
3 tsp. Worcestershire sauce   finely chopped chives
Cream butter until light and lemon colored with mustard,
Worcestershire sauce, Tabasco sauce, onion and chives. Blend
thoroughly and chill.

Garlic Butter:
1 clove ground garlic   1 Tbsp. salted butter
Mix blanched and dried garlic with salted butter. Chill
well.

221 MEXICAN APPETIZER
1 can bean dip   1/4 c. minced onion
1 mashed avocado (add a few   1 jar mild taco sauce
drops lemon juice)   1 (8 oz.) carton sour cream
1/4 c. chopped black olives
Top with grated Cheddar cheese and garnish with cherry tomatoes.

222 PINWHEEL APPETIZERS
3 chicken breasts, cooked   1 green onion, chopped fine
8 oz. cream cheese, softened   1 c. grated Cheddar cheese
1 small can diced green   large flour tortillas
chilies

Skin, debone and chop fine the cooked chicken breasts. Combine all
ingredients, except tortillas. Spread mixture on tortillas. Roll up
tortillas. Refrigerate, covered, for 5 hours or overnight. Slice 1/4-inch
thick.

223 JALAPENO SQUARES
7 to 8 chopped jalapenos   6 eggs

1 to 1 1/2 lb. sharp   cheese,shredded

Grease a 9-inch baking pan. Spread jalapenos over bottom of dish. Cover with cheese. Beat 6 eggs and pour over other ingredients. Bake at 350 degrees for 25 to 30 minutes or until set. Cut into squares and serve. Small squares make a tasty appetizer; cut larger squares for an entree. Makes 25 appetizer squares.

224 SHRIMP HERBED JALAPENO CHEESE

2 lb. unpeeled large fresh	1 clove garlic, minced
shrimp	2 pickled jalapeno peppers,
6 c. water	seeded, finely chopped
1/2 tsp. salt	2 tsp. dried cilantro
1 (8 oz.) pkg. cream cheese,	salt and pepper to taste
softened	

Peel shrimp, leaving tail and first joint of shell intact. Cut a deep slit down the length of the outside curve of each shrimp and de-vein. Combine water and salt in a large saucepan. Bring to a boil. Add shrimp and cook 3 to 5 minutes. Drain well; rinse in cold water. Pat dry. Chill. Combine cheese and remaining ingredients; beat well. Fill a decorating bag fitted with metal tip #21 with cream cheese mixture. Pipe filling lengthwise into slits in the shrimp.

225 NACHO CHEESE DIP

1 lb. Velveeta cheese	1 medium onion
1 (8 oz.) pkg. cream cheese	1/2 stick butter
1 (16 oz.) can whole tomatoes	1/2 to 3/4 c. jalapeno peppers

First heat. Cook oleo, peppers and onions (cut small) in microwave oven for about 4 minutes until soft. Second crush tomatoes. Third melt both cheeses together in medium size bowl in microwave, stirring occasionally. Fourth combine all ingredients. Serve as a dip with tortilla chips. Makes a great appetizer and a party favorite!

226 FRESH VEGETABLES WITH GUACAMOLE DIP

2 small avocados	2 red peppers, cut into thin
2 Tbsp. lemon juice	strips
2 Tbsp. chopped green onions	2 (8 oz.) bags or bunches
2 tsp. salt	white radishes, cut into thin
1 tsp. sugar	slices
1/2 tsp. hot pepper sauce	2 green peppers, cut into thin
dash of pepper	slices

About 2 hours before serving, or early in the morning prepare guacamole. In covered blender container, at medium speed, blend avocados, lemon juice, green onions, salt, sugar, hot pepper sauce and dash of pepper until smooth, stopping blender occasionally and scraping sides of container with rubber spatula. Spoon guacamole into small bowl; cover and refrigerate until well chilled. To serve: Arrange vegetables and guacamole on platter.

227 SALMON AND SOLE TERRINE WITH DILL SAUCE

Terrine:

12 oz. sole fillets
6 oz. salmon
2 c. heavy cream
1 1/2 to 2 tsp. salt

1 1/2 tsp. ground red chili peppers
1/4 c. fresh lemon juice

Dill Sauce:

1/2 c. sour cream (or plain yogurt)
1/2 c. mayonnaise
1/4 c. fresh lemon juice
2 pinches cayenne pepper

1/4 tsp. salt
pepper to taste
1 small bunch fresh dill, chopped (no stems)

Preheat oven to 425 degrees. Place terrine ingredients in food processor and blend until smooth. Pour into small 3-inch deep buttered loaf pan. Place loaf pan into large pan with boiling water (double boiler) and bake for 30 minutes. Cool and un-mold. Place all sauce ingredients in processor and blend until smooth.

228 ROAST PEPPERS

8 medium-sized sweet red peppers
1 c. olive or salad oil
1/4 c. lemon juice

2 tsp. salt
3 small cloves garlic
3 anchovy fillets

Preheat oven to 450 degrees. Wash and drain peppers well. Place peppers on cookie sheet; bake 20 minutes or until skins of peppers become blistered and charred. Turn every 5 minutes with tongs. Place hot peppers in large kettle; cover. Let the peppers stand 15 to 20 minutes. Peel off charred skin with sharp knife. Cut each pepper into fourths. Remove ribs and seeds. Cut out any dark spots. In large bowl, combine olive oil, lemon juice, salt and garlic. Add pepper quarters and toss lightly to coat. Pack pepper mixture along with anchovies into a 1 quart jar; cap. Refrigerate several hours or overnight. Serve as appetizer or in a tossed salad.

229 BROILED POTATO SKINS

4 large baking potatoes
1/2 tsp. salt

4 slices bacon, crisply cooked and crumbled

1 c. finely shredded Monterey	peppers (4 oz.)
Jack cheese with jalapeno	2 Tbsp. butter

Prick potatoes with fork to allow steam to escape. Bake potatoes in 425 degrees oven until tender, about 1 hour. Cool slightly. Cut each potato lengthwise into halves. Scoop out insides leaving a 3/8 inch shell. Spread inside of shells with butter; sprinkle with salt. Cut each into 6 pieces; sprinkle with cheese and bacon. Set oven control to broiler 550 degrees. Broil potato pieces with tops about 5 inches from heat until cheese is melted, about 2 minutes. Makes 48 appetizers.

230 CARROT APPETIZER

3 lb. carrots	1/2 c. oil
2 onions	1/2 c. sugar
3 green peppers	1/4 c. vinegar
1 can tomato soup	salt and pepper

Cook 3 pounds of carrots and slice round. Slice onions and green pepper. Mix 1 can tomato soup and 1/2 cup oil. Add 1/2 cup sugar, salt, pepper and 1/4 cup vinegar. Marinate for one day.

231 SHRIMP IN MUSTARD SAUCE

2 1/2 lb. cooked shrimp	4 Tbsp. Dijon mustard
1/4 c. chopped parsley	2 tsp. crushed red peppers
1/4 c. chopped shallots	2 tsp. salt
1/4 c. tarragon vinegar	1 Tbsp. sugar
1/4 c. red wine vinegar	ground pepper
1/2 c. olive oil	

Cook shrimp until pink. Pour remaining ingredients over warm shrimp. Mix well. Cover and refrigerate overnight.

232 PIMENTO CHEESE SPREAD

1 (8 oz.) pkg. cream cheese,	1 c. green onions
softened	1 to 1 1/2 c. mayonnaise
3 eggs, boiled	salt and pepper to taste
1 jar pimento	paprika to taste
2 medium bell peppers	

Beat cream cheese until creamy. Chop eggs and pimento. Chop very fine bell pepper and green onions. Mix all ingredients together. Blend well; chill. Serve as spread on crackers or for stuffing celery sticks as an appetizer.

233 PIZZA SALAD APPETIZER

1 pkg. crescent roll dough	1 c. shredded American
1 lb. cream cheese	cheese
1 c. black and green olives	

1 qt. assorted cut green vegetables (cauliflower, broccoli, cherry tomatoes, peppers, etc.)

Bake dough according to directions in baking dish large enough to provide uniform 1/2-inch crust. When crust is baked, let cool, then spread cream cheese uniformly over entire surface. Top the cheese with the assorted vegetables and olives and finally sprinkle the shredded cheese over the vegetables. Refrigerate for 2 hours and serve in 2-inch squares.

234   TACO DIP

1 (8 oz.) jar mayonnaise
1 sour cream
1 package ranch dressing dry mix
1 (8 oz.) cream cheese
1 pkg. shredded Cheddar cheese
1/2 lb. hamburger
1 jar taco sauce
1/2 head lettuce, shredded
1 pepper, chopped
3 small tomatoes, chopped

Combine mayonnaise, sour cream, dry ranch dressing mix and cream cheese. Mix well. Divide in half. Use one portion for this time. Save the other for another time. Brown hamburger in 2 tablespoons taco sauce. While this is browning, spread 1st mixture onto serving tray. Smooth taco sauce on top. Add hamburger, lettuce, tomatoes, peppers and cheese. Keep refrigerated. Serve with nacho chips or crackers.

235 MEXICAN SALAD

1/4 c. chopped bell peppers
1 c. grated sharp cheese
1/4 c. chopped green onions
1 tsp. Tabasco sauce
1 bottle Green Goddess dressing
1 c. chopped tomatoes
1 c. grated Mozzarella cheese
1 c. grated Cheddar cheese

Mix all ingredients together in a large bowl. Let chill in refrigerator for 1 hour. Serve with nacho chips.

236 PEPPERS STUFFED WITH PORK AND HERBS

6 firm green peppers
boiling water to cover
4 Tbsp. (1/2 stick) butter
1/2 c. finely chopped onion
1 clove garlic, finely minced
1 1/2 lb. lean ground pork
1/2 lb. mushrooms, chopped
1 1/2 c. fresh bread crumbs
salt and freshly ground black pepper to taste
2 Tbsp. finely chopped parsley
1/2 tsp. finely chopped rosemary
1/4 c. grated Parmesan cheese
1/4 c. water or tomato sauce

Preheat the oven to 350 degrees. Cut a slice off the stem ends of the peppers and discard it. Using the fingers and a paring knife, carefully pare away the white pith inside the peppers. Shake out the seeds. Have a kettle ready with enough boiling water in it to cover the peppers. Drop in the peppers and let them cook for 5 minutes. Drain them immediately in a colander. In a large skillet melt the butter and cook the onion and garlic until onion is wilted. Add the pork and cook, breaking up the meat with a slotted spoon. Cover until the pork loses color. Add the mushrooms and cook, stirring for 3 minutes more. Add the bread crumbs, salt, pepper, parsley and rosemary. Spoon equal amounts of the mixture into the pepper cases. Sprinkle equal amounts of cheese onto the stuffing and arrange the peppers in a baking dish. Pour the water or tomato sauce around them and bake until peppers are tender, about 25 minutes.

Please do not call the author or publisher with questions about cooking or where to buy peppers (or other ingredients) in your hometown. We suggest you use your telephone directory to locate produce stores, and visit your library if you want to know what particular ingredients are. To learn more about Native American or Hispanic cuisine, we suggest you take classes at your local community education centers or watch the food channel. The internet is an excellent source for finding seeds which you can plant to grow a large variety of peppers.

To join Anton's fan club, visit http://groups.yahoo.com/group/Anton

This book, Anton's Festive Salsas is available from Amazon.com for $14.95 plus shipping and handling.

Anton's

Festive Salsas

Thank you for purchasing a copy of this book. Here's a special offer for promotional copies of <u>Anton's Festive Salsas</u> at a special price to give to your friends.

Send $10 per book, plus $2 flat rate for shipping regardless of the number of copies ordered. On your check's memo area write promotional code "Salsa Special" and make check payable to Anton Anderssen. You will receive your book from the author's promotional printings, and therefore they could be very slightly different from this book (e.g. no bar code or price printed on the cover, etc.) Stock may be limited. Will ship whenever promotional copies become available. Mail to

Anton Anderssen   4177 Garrick Ave
Warren Mi 48091

Please do not make any shipping inquiries until you are certain your check has cleared your bank.